Did **Adam & Eve** **B**elly **Have** **Buttons?**

And **199** other questions from Catholic teenagers

Matthew J. Pinto

 DynamicCatholic.com
Be Bold. Be Catholic.

Nihil obstat: Rev. Joseph G. Prior
                   Censor Librorum
                   June 29, 2003

Imprimatur: +Anthony Cardinal Bevilaqua
                   Archbishop of Philadelphia
                   June 30, 2003

Published by Beacon Publishing
with permission from Ascension Press.

Ascension Press
Post Office Box 1990
West Chester, PA 19380
www.AscensionPress.com
Orders: 1-800-376-0520

For more information about this title and other books and CDs available
through the Dynamic Catholic Book Program, please visit:
www.DynamicCatholic.com

Cover design: Kinsey Caruth

Published in the United States of America

ISBN 978-0-9659228-8-3

To my wife, Maryanne.
Thank you for your steadfast love and support.
You are a gift from God.

Prayer Before Reading

Come Holy Spirit, fill the hearts of Your faithful
And enkindle in them the fire of Your love.
Send forth Your Spirit and they shall be created,
And You shall renew the face of the earth.

O God, who did instruct the hearts of the faithful
By the light of the Holy Spirit,
Grant us by the same Spirit to have a right judgment
In all things and ever to rejoice in His consolation.
Through Christ our Lord.
Amen.

Contents

Foreword

There is no doubt about it. Young people today are on a quest for truth and happiness, and I believe they are seeing that they will find them only in God (CCC 27). Nearly every day someone calls or writes me requesting a dynamic book for teens that will lead them to God. Parents want a book to give their teens that will help them answer life's difficult questions in a format teens can appreciate. Teens want a book they can give to their friends with inquiring hearts. *Did Adam and Eve Have Belly Buttons?* is just such a book.

Teens today are faced with more complex questions than were past generations. At the same time, distinguishing truth from falsehood in our popular culture is increasingly difficult as trendsetters speak (and act) as if nothing is "black and white," only shades of gray. Even more dangerous yet, the messages and techniques of Church youth leaders often cannot be distinguished from those of secular humanism or the New Age movement.

The simplicity and clarity of this book's style and content will be refreshing to those who have to continually battle for the truth in their own backyard. What makes *Did Adam and Eve Have Belly Buttons?* so relevant and useful is that the questions included are real questions submitted by real teens. The author, Matthew Pinto, doesn't shy away from difficult topics and gives straightforward answers that are in harmony with Church teaching. Answers include citations from the Bible and the *Catechism of the Catholic Church.* Readers will appreciate both the scope of the questions and the succinct answers.

This handy tool will help young Catholics understand and defend their faith. Most importantly, it will better equip them to live holy lives consecrated to Jesus Christ. This book is valuable for personal or group study. It can be used as a reference tool for evangelization and as an aid to youth leaders in their lesson preparation.

Those who personally know the author are impressed with his energy and enthusiasm in working with young people. Matt Pinto knows how teens think and what social and spiritual situations they face. As a popular youth speaker, he is a master at applying the truths of the Church to the ever-changing moral and social landscape. Now he brings his energy, enthusiasm, and skills to the written page.

So begin the journey. If you are a teenager, read with an open mind. Then, if you are inspired and convinced by the answers, act on them by becoming a soldier for the Lord. If you are a parent or teacher, read this book yourself and pass it on. The answers contained within are for all.

—Jeff Cavins, Creator
The Great Adventure
Bible Study program

Introduction

I started my own advertising business fresh out of college. I wanted success *and I wanted it quickly.* Working sixty to seventy hours a week for the first three years, the fruits of my labor began to show. I was on my way to wealth and recognition at a young age.

But then something unexpected happened—I was growing disconcerted with the way my life was going. Living only for personal gain, I felt empty and shallow. I was burning out at the ripe old age of twenty-four.

I turned to my Catholic faith to fill the void. I searched out a young adult group at a nearby parish, and it was there that I crashed head-on into Catholic truth. Dynamic young Catholics showed me there was more to life than material gain. I learned that I could gain the whole world and lose my soul in the process (Mk 8:36).

I wasted no time embracing the faith. Intense about most things, I began an aggressive study of Christianity. That first year I must have read or studied more than a thousand hours. I replaced my time-management and motivational tapes with theological ones by the late Bishop Fulton Sheen and other Catholic teachers. I even stopped dating to clear my mind from all distractions. I was "on fire."

For the first time in my life I knew who I was. I was a

child of God, a Christian, a CATHOLIC! I no longer felt a void in my life. My identity, confidence, and purpose were firmly established. A short time later, I sold my business to work full-time for the Church.

Why tell you all this? Because, since then, I have seen many conversions similar to my own. Through my involvement with youth and young adult ministry, I have seen hundreds of teens and young adults come to the same surety of faith. All they needed was to be introduced to the powerful, life-changing teachings of Jesus Christ and His Church. The faith was not "watered down." These teens and young adults were taught clear Catholic truth and they responded enthusiastically.

Contrary to popular belief, young people do not run away from the Church's "tough" teachings (or get bored in religious education class) when Catholic truth is presented clearly and with conviction. Young Catholics are looking for a rock on which to stand, a firm foundation in an ever-changing world. The Catholic faith offers this rock-solid foundation.

Without a correct understanding of Catholic truth our young Catholics will founder. They will be unsure who they are and about what they stand for. They will remain silent at dinner parties when Uncle Louie badmouths the Church. They will not speak up when their friends promote premarital sex or abortion, and they will have no answers to the non-Catholic missionaries who come knocking on their door.

With a little training in *apologetics* (the art of defending and giving reasons for one's beliefs), Catholic youth *will* speak up. They will be ready to explain, share, and charitably defend the faith. They will be able to "give reasons for the hope that is within them" (1 Pt 3:15).

This is a book of Catholic apologetics. It is composed of serious questions from actual teenagers, including (believe it or not) the question forming the book's title. I have attempted to give each question a serious answer and to present Catholic teaching in a clear manner. By learning and living the truth, our young people will be set free from the "spirit of the age" (Jn 8:12) and have to live more abundant lives (Jn 10:10).

The format of this book makes it an easy read. You can read it straight through or "hop around" to the questions that most interest you. Share it with your youth group, parish RCIA, or religious education class.

Pray before you read. If you are sincerely seeking the truth, God will lead you to it. Simply ask and He will respond (Mt 7:7).

—Matthew J. Pinto

Key to Biblical Abbreviations

The following abbreviations are used for the various Scriptural verses cited throughout the book. (*Note*: CCC = *Catechism of the Catholic Church*.)

Old Testament

Gn	Genesis	Jon	Jonah
Ex	Exodus	Mi	Micah
Lv	Leviticus	Na	Nahum
Nm	Numbers	Hb	Habakkuk
Dt	Deuteronomy	Zep	Zephaniah
Jos	Joshua	Hg	Haggai
Jgs	Judges	Zec	Zechariah
Ru	Ruth	Mal	Malachi
1 Sam	1 Samuel		
2 Sam	2 Samuel		
1 Kgs	1 Kings		**New Testament**
2 Kgs	2 Kings	Mt	Matthew
1 Chr	1 Chronicles 2	Mk	Mark
Chr	2 Chronicles	Lk	Luke
Ezr	Ezra	Jn	John
Neh	Nehemiah	Acts	Acts
Tb	Tobit	Rom	Romans
Jdt	Judith	1 Cor	1 Corinthians
Est	Esther	2 Cor	2 Corinthians
1 Mc	1 Maccabees	Gal	Galatians
2 Mc	2 Maccabees	Eph	Ephesians
Jb	Job	Phil	Philippians
Ps	Psalms	Col	Colossians
Prv	Proverbs	1 Thess	1 Thessalonians
Eccl	Ecclesiastes	2 Thess	2 Thessalonians
Sng	Song of Songs	1 Tm	1 Timothy
Wis	Wisdom	2 Tm	2 Timothy
Sir	Sirach	Ti	Titus
Is	Isaiah	Phlm	Philemon
Jer	Jeremiah	Heb	Hebrews
Lam	Lamentations	Jas	James
Bar	Baruch	1 Pt	1 Peter
Ez	Ezekiel	2 Pt	2 Peter
Dn	Daniel	1 Jn	1 John
Hos	Hosea	2 Jn	2 John
Jl	Joel	3 Jn	3 John
Am	Amos	Jude	Jude
Ob	Obadiah	Rv	Revelation

Chapter 1
GOD

Question #1

"Is there really a God?" Stephen C., 15

A. Yes. God is the ultimate reality. He is actually holding all things in existence (Col 1:17; Heb 1:3). If God stopped doing so, we would cease to exist, but He would continue to exist (Ps 90:1–10).

We know God exists through revelation (Heb 1:1–2), which comes to us through Scripture and Sacred Tradition, and by our own intellects (Rom 1:19–20; Ps 19:2–5; CCC 31, 34). Sacred Tradition includes the truths of the Catholic faith passed on by the apostles, which were not necessarily committed to writing. It is the common life, worship, and teaching of the Body of Christ, in union with the successors of the apostles, the bishops, and the successor of Peter, the pope.

In the Bible, God reveals: "I Am" (Ex 3:14) and "I am the Alpha and the Omega" (Rev 1:8), which means He is the beginning and end of all things. God also has some harsh words for those who deny He exists: "The fool says in his heart that there is no God" (Ps 14:1, 53:2).

Question #2

"Other than the Bible, how do we know God exists?" Travis C., 14

A. St. Thomas Aquinas says we can know of God by reason alone. He gives five demonstrations of the existence of God. I will give you one of them and then challenge you to read St. Thomas' works to find out the other four (see St. Thomas' masterpiece *Summa Theologica*—or check out the helpful companion book *A Tour of the Summa*, a summary of St. Thomas' thoughts, published by TAN Books).

One proof or argument is from "design." This proof says the universe could not have just come together on its own any more than, say, a computer just "comes together" on its own (CCC 33, 34). The computer is a precise instrument that could not magically come together by random chance. It is created and designed by something greater than itself—man. But if man is vastly *more* complex than the computer, what is the sense of saying he is simply the product of wind and weather? If the computer is the obvious creation of a human mind, the human mind is an even more obvious creation of a divine mind.

So we know God exists by His handiwork (Ps 19:2). Only an all-powerful God could have orchestrated the creation of the universe, the earth, man, and everything else (Is 44:24; Job 38:4–39:30).

Question #3

"Who is God?" Jan Rio P., 14

A. God is our Father. God is our Creator, our Redeemer, and our Sanctifier. God is the Blessed Trinity—three distinct Persons who share the same divine nature. God is an eternal family. God is truth (Ps 119:160; CCC 215). God is love (1 Jn 4:8,16; CCC 221).

Question #4

"What is the nature of God?" Nathan T., 15

A. God is the Supreme Being. He is self-existing (not caused) (Jn 1:1–3), eternal (Ps 90:1–10, 102:25), all-powerful (Mt 19:26; CCC 268), all-knowing (Ps 139:1–18; Job 28:24; Sir 39:20) and present everywhere (Jer 23:24).

God is pure spirit (Jn 4:24), which means He does not have the limitations of a body. God is also supremely personal (Jer 1:4–5; Jn 3:16; CCC 203). He is no mere force or power. In fact, He is a communion of Persons—Father, Son, and Holy Spirit (Mt 28:19; 2 Cor 13:13). This is the Blessed Trinity. All three Persons possess the one divine nature (Rom 15:6; Jn 20:28; CCC 242) yet are distinct.

Question #5

"What made God so great?" Maria B., 14

A. Strictly speaking, nothing "made" God great. This question is like asking, "What was before time?" There is no time before time, so you cannot talk about "before" and "after" time. The same holds true here. God made everything. Every beautiful thing you love, every work of art or nature, every majestic mountain range, every hero you have ever admired, every moment you have ever cherished in your memory—all the awesome or breathtaking things you have ever experienced are just dim reflections of their Creator. He is not "like" those things. Those things are a little bit like Him, for He is their Author (Gn 1).

Question #6

"What does God look like?" Rachel P., 13

A. God the Father is a pure spirit, which means He has no body (Jn 4:24). We cannot describe then what He "looks like," because that phrase assumes God the Father has a body like ours that we could "look at" (Jn 1:18).

Because it is hard for us to think of a being without a body, God has given us images or descriptions of Himself that help us picture what He is like. For example, we can think of God as a loving Father who cares for and cherishes His children (Mt 6:9; Lk 11:11–13).

The best "picture" of God, however, is Jesus Himself, who said, "Whoever has seen me has seen the Father" (Jn 14:9). As God the Son, Jesus showed us what God the Father is like. He also showed us the Father's perfect love by teaching people (Lk 5:3; Mk 10:1), healing the sick (Mt 9:27–30; Lk 4:40), forgiving sins (Lk 5:17–25) and, most of all, dying for our sins on the cross (Jn 19:30; Phil 2:8).

Jesus promised us that if we love God, one day we will see Him in the beatific vision, which means that our hearts and minds will be perfectly united with God in heaven (Mk 12:28–34; Jn 14:21–23; CCC 2548). In this "vision of God," we will be completely happy and at peace: We will want nothing (1 Cor 2:9; Rv 21:1–4; CCC 2550).

Question #7

"How did God create Himself?" John D., 14

A. He didn't create himself. He has always existed.

Creation means to make something from nothing. To create something requires that the creator exist before the thing created. When a carpenter makes a table, for example, he exists before the table he makes. For God to create himself, He would have to exist before Himself, which does not make any sense.

God could not have been created by someone else, because then God's creator would be greater than God. And that does not make sense because God is the Supreme (or highest) Being, and you cannot go any higher than the highest.

When Moses asked God at the burning bush what His name was, He responded "I Am who Am" (Ex 3:14), which indicates that God is existence (or "being") itself.

Question #8

"What does the Church mean when it refers to God as 'the Father'?" Rocky P., 15

A. The Church means that, although God is a pure spirit and not literally male, we speak of God in masculine terms because God's relation to us is like that of a father (CCC 239). This does not mean men are better than women, only that some aspects of "maleness" better express some aspects of God's relationship to us than "femaleness." Both men and women are made in God's image (Gn 1:27).

One reason the Church calls God "Father" is Jesus. Our relation to God is a sharing in Jesus' relation to God. He knew and revealed God as Father (Mt 11:27; CCC 240). In fact, He said, "When you pray, say 'Father'" (Lk 11:2).

Therefore, that is how we should know and relate to God. Jesus could not know God as Mother for a simple reason: He already had a Mother, the Blessed Virgin Mary (Lk 2:7; CCC 509). As Jesus' brothers and sisters, we too have Mary as our spiritual Mother (Jn 19:25–27; CCC 501). And God is our spiritual Father, a fatherhood more real than even our biological relationship with our own earthly fathers (1 Jn 3:1).

Another reason we call God "Father" has to do with His relation to us as His creatures (Rom 8:15–17, 22–23; CCC 238). God the Father bestows seeds of grace to the Church, within which we are nurtured as a spiritual womb. Thus, the Church has traditionally been called "Holy Mother Church" and referred to as "she."

The *Catechism of the Catholic Church* states that God's Fatherhood includes the perfections of human fatherhood and motherhood. And the Bible also sometimes describes God's love in maternal ways (Is 49:15, 66:13). So we should not be afraid of all maternal imagery as a way of understanding God's love for us, provided it is properly understood. However, neither the Bible nor the *Catechism* ever calls God "mother." And even when maternal images are used in the Bible, God remains "He" not "She" (CCC 239).

Naturally, there is much more, but this overview should give you at least a basic understanding of this important issue.

Question #9

"How do I know that God loves me?" Kyle T., 14

A. Because He made you in His image and likeness, which He did not have to do (Gn 1:26–27). Quite simply, God made you because He loves you and knew you would like it (CCC 1604). God needs no companions. He does not need our praise. His creation of us was a gift (Acts 17:24–25). His love for you is pure because He doesn't need to use you to get something for Himself. There are no strings attached to His love, no hidden agendas.

He also made you because He wants you to experience the bliss and unspeakable joy that will come from spending eternity with Him (Jn 4:7–15, 14:2–3; Rv 21:1–4; CCC 1). And He will do everything he can to bestow eternal life on us, with the exception of forcing us to love and obey Him.

We also know God loves us because Scripture says, "God so loved the world that He sent His only Son so that everyone who believes in Him might not perish but might have eternal life" (Jn 3:16; CCC 458). If He had not given His Son as the ultimate sacrifice for sin, we all would have perished because of sin (Col 2:13–14; Heb 5:8–9). Sending His Son was an act of love (Jn 15:13; Rom 5:8, 8:32).

Question #10

"Will God always love you no matter what you do?" Kindra M., 16

A. Yes, but this does not mean you will get to heaven no matter what you do. A parent who loves a teenager too much to let him live a destructive life may kick the teenager out of the house. If the teen does not seek forgiveness, he may never be allowed back.

This is not a perfect analogy (because God does not "kick us out" of heaven; we choose to be separated from Him), but it helps demonstrate the point that God does not force salvation on us. He gives us free will to either accept or reject His love (Rv 3:20; Sir 15:17; CCC 1730). However, He does continually send us grace to work on our hearts and consciences, because it is His will that all be saved (1 Tm 2:4; CCC 74).

If we do not want to be saved and prove this by disobedience, we will not be saved (Jn 3:36). This does not mean that God does not love us. He loves us more than we can know (Rom 8:35–39). However, salvation is conditional, based on our response to His love (Mt 25:31–46; Jn 14:21–24; CCC 2002). Why? Because "salvation" ultimately means being with God (Rv 21:1–4, 22:3–4), and God will not force anyone to be with Him who does not want to be with Him (Rv 3:20).

Question #11

"How can God change my life?" Ed R., 17

A. God made you (Gn 1:27; CCC 1). He knows everything you ever did or will do (Rom 8:29–30; CCC 257). He knows you better than you know yourself. Scripture says He even knows the number of hairs on your head (Lk 12:7). By humbling ourselves and asking for His guidance, He will lead us to peace and happiness in this life and eternal joy in the next (Rom 10:9–10, 13).

Not allowing God to work in your life is like swimming upstream—you simply will not get anywhere that really counts (1 Sam 2:9). All achievements will be in vain. However, with God every action has a purpose (Rom 8:28; CCC 313, 395).

Question #12

"If God cares for people, how come He lets people kill each other?" Lauren S., 15

A. For the same reason He lets people love each other. He loved us so much that He gave us the tremendous gift of free will (Sir 15:11-17).

God wants human beings to choose Him freely. He does not want to force Himself on us (Rv 3:20). God gave us wills so we would be able to experience some of the joy He knows as God. This joy comes from the divine love, and this type of love requires freedom (Jos 24:15). (Freedom involves the ability to freely give one's self to another.) Not even God can force us to love Him because the words "force" and "love" are mutually contradictory.

Man cannot be free to love God without having, at the same time, the freedom to reject Him (Prv 1:29-30; CCC 1730). With this freedom comes the possibility of evil, which God hates but does allow. It is this free will that enables some people to embrace evil (Gn 4:7-8; CCC 1732, 2259). This can lead to sin, including murder, even mass murder. Rest assured, however, that neither iniquities nor injustices will go unpunished in the eternal courtroom (Mt 12:36-37; Rom 2:6-11).

Question #13

"Why does God make us suffer from abuse and diseases like cancer?" Caity N., 14

A. God does not create abuse and disease, but He sometimes *permits* them.

Evil is a mystery; we can never understand it completely. But this does not mean we cannot understand anything about it (CCC 309, 314).

To begin to think about evil, we need to first think about God and what he has revealed. God has one ultimate will, but this will is expressed in two ways: His *positive* will and His *permissive* will. His positive will is what brings about all the good we see.

God's permissive will *allows* evil to happen but only because He intends to bring about a greater good from it (CCC 312). Often, evil is a result of man's free choices (Prv 1:29–30; CCC 1732). God simply allows the natural consequences that inevitably flow from these choices. Even so, God can always bring greater good from this (Rom 8:28).

Much good can come from suffering if we embrace it when it comes our way (Rom 8:18; CCC 1501, 1502). Let's say a man has lived a very selfish life that includes heavy drinking and abuse of his wife. God may allow this man to lose his health because He knows that if the man stays healthy, he will continue to sin. If the man is incapacitated, however, he may come to see the true beauty of his wife and then reconcile himself to God and his wife.

One final point: God understands our suffering through the suffering of Christ on the cross (Heb 2:18). We can link our sufferings with the sufferings of Jesus on the cross and, thus, offer them up as gifts to the Father (2 Cor 1:5; Col 1:24; CCC 1508).

Chapter 2

CREATION AND MAN

Question #14

"What is the meaning of life?" Zed R., 13

A. The meaning of life is to know, love, and serve God (Jn 17:3; Sir 1:11–12; CCC 356, 357, 1721). This is where we will find our fulfillment here on earth and in heaven (Rom 15:13; Jn 17:13; CCC 1718). Love is the underlying theme throughout the Bible (1 Jn 4:8; Jn 3:16). In fact, there are more than six hundred verses in Scripture that speak explicitly of love.

To begin, the creation of human beings was an act of unselfish love by God. He did not need us because He is perfect (Job 35:5–7; Acts 17:24–25) and needs nothing. But He created us because He knew we would like it (Gn 1:26–31). This was an act of love. God exhibited the ultimate act of love when He gave His only Son as the definitive sacrifice to save the world from its sins (Jn 3:16). The Son, Jesus Christ, gave His own life for us when He died on the cross (2 Cor 5:14–15; Heb 2:9; Phil 2:5–8).

We are called to this type of unselfish love (1 Jn 4:19). Love is most fully expressed when we give of ourselves with no interest in gaining something from it (1 Cor 13:5; CCC 2196). Love is wanting what is best for another *simply because it is best for that person.* Love is the greatest of the virtues (1 Cor 13:13). Love is the opposite of selfishness (Rom 13:8–10). Love truly makes the world a better place (1 Cor 13:4–7). Without love, we have only emptiness.

The meaning of life is love: Accepting love from God, giving love back to God through obedience to Him, and loving others as we love God and ourselves (1 Jn 4:19; Jn 13:34–35, 14:15, 15:12–17; CCC 1823).

Question #15

"Did God make the whole world? If not, how did the world begin?" Rachel P., 13

A. Yes, God made the whole world (Gn 1–2:2). But God did not merely *make* the world. He *created* it from nothing (2 Mc 7:28). A carpenter makes a chair from wood. A poet makes a poem from words that already exist. Making something implies that the original materials are there first. Although we speak of people *creating*, only God creates in the strictest sense, for only God can bring something from nothing (CCC 296).

God alone brought the universe into existence from nothing (Jn 1:1–3; CCC 317). He creates each and every human soul from nothing at conception (Jer 1:5).

Why did God create the universe from nothing rather than something? Well, what else would He have created it from? Not from Himself, for there are no parts in God that He could "break off" to fashion things from. And if He used something else, where would *that* have come from?

God is all-powerful. He can do what no one else can: create something from nothing (Gn 1:1; CCC 298). Scripture says: "He spoke and they were made. He commanded and they were created" (Ps 148:5; CCC 297).

Question #16

"Doesn't the Big Bang Theory explain the way the world was created apart from a Creator?"
Tracy P., 18

A. No, because even if the Big Bang Theory is true, it does not explain where the matter came from that caused the Big Bang. And even if you hold, as some scientists do, that before the Big Bang that started our universe there were an infinite number of Big Bangs and Big Collapses (or "earlier" universes), you still have a problem: Where did the stuff these Big Bangs and Big Collapses were made of come from? Also, why is the universe the kind of place where there are such occurrences? It doesn't have to be. Where did the whole thing come from, anyway?

Since the universe does not explain its own existence, the explanation for it must be somewhere else; actually in *Someone* else, the one who is self-existing: God (Is 45:11–12).

Note: You will sometimes hear people say that there is a conflict between science and religion, between reason and faith. These people believe that science has "debunked" or disproved religious beliefs and replaced them with the "real" truth. The Big Bang Theory is one example of this mentality, and people often argue that it disproves God's creation of the universe. But as we said above, it does nothing of the sort. Science and religion are not opposed to each other, if their proper roles are correctly understood. Science, which takes its conclusions from data collected by observation and measurement, is very good at answering the "how" questions. But it is not equipped to answer the "why" questions. For example, it cannot tell us why we are here or what the purpose of life is.

Question #17

"If the sun and the moon mark the days and they were created on the fourth day, how could the other days have come about?" Nicholas D., 14

A. Your question shows one of the problems with accepting the Genesis story as a complete, literal scientific history of creation. Of course, much of the Book of Genesis is historical—the existence of Abraham, for example. But the Catholic faith allows us to interpret other parts of it figuratively, as long as our interpretations do not contradict other Catholic doctrines (CCC 390).

As Catholics, we are not forced into the restrictive interpretations of the creation presented by some Protestant fundamentalists. For example, we do not have to assume that all narratives in the opening chapters of Genesis are strictly historical, or historical in every detail, in order to believe that there was a creation and fall of man. When we think of the writer of Genesis as expressing the creation of the world in poetic fashion, the problem you mention vanishes.

According to Genesis 1, God created light and distinguished light and darkness on the "first day." This "day," however, is not so much a twenty-four hour period as a poetic way of showing how God created things in stages, in an orderly fashion, fitting each thing in its proper place (1 Cor 14:40). After God created "light," for instance, He then created realms or places for things: the sky, separating it from the waters covering the earth; and the oceans, separating them from dry land (Gn 1:6–13). Finally, He populated these places with things: first, plants on the land, then sun, moon, and stars in the sky; and then sea creatures and birds (Gn 1:14–23). On the final "day" of creation, God created the land animals and, after this, man (Gn 1:24–31).

As the Genesis writer describes it, God went from the most basic creatures to the highest, most complex— man, made in God's image—creating a place for each beforehand. This shows in a poetic form, rather than in a strictly scientific description, that God created things in an orderly fashion because He is a God of order, not chaos (1 Cor 14:33).

So the historical truth of the Genesis creation story is one thing: God *did* create the world and man. How that truth is recounted, poetically, is another (CCC 198).

Question #18

"Did Adam and Eve have belly buttons?"
Gilbert A., 18

A. Your fellow teens may think this is a joke question, but it actually is very clever. You are really asking, "If Adam and Eve were created directly by God, they should *not* have belly buttons. But if they evolved from apes, wouldn't they have had belly buttons?"

Quite frankly, we just do not know if Adam and Eve had belly buttons. The Church does not speak of whether they did or did not have them, because it does not speak officially on *how* creation took place. The Church is mainly concerned with *why* creation took place and *what* the implications of our creation are (CCC 1).

So, although this may be a clever title for a book, we just don't know the answer for sure. You will have to wait until you get to heaven to find out (1 Cor 13:12; CCC 314). (Note: This is one of the few "We don't know" answers in this book.)

Of course, God could have created Adam and Eve with belly buttons, just as He may have created them mature, rather than as children. Instead of asking whether or not they had belly buttons, perhaps we should ponder an even more profound question: "If they did have belly buttons, would they have been 'innies' or 'outies'?"

Question #19

"Can a Catholic believe in evolution?"
Rebecca G., 17

A. Looking at evolution as the process of *how* God created the world does not pose a problem for the Catholic. However, because some aspects of "evolution" can impact the faith of the believer, the Church does offer guidelines for what must be believed and what is left up to the individual's judgment.

Before considering those guidelines, let's be clear about the difference between "evolution" and "evolutionism." Evolution is a scientific *theory* that says that more complex forms of life developed from less complex forms, over extremely long periods of time (perhaps a couple of billion years). As a scientific theory, it is to be accepted or rejected based on the evidence.

Evolution*ism*, on the other hand, is the belief that everything that exists can be explained in exclusively materialist terms, apart from a Creator. According to evolutionism, everything that exists developed from "blind chance," with no knowing or planning of its purpose or end.

Evolutionism is not only unscientific; it is unreasonable. A complex organism like the human brain could not have developed by "blind chance." Because evolutionism denies the creative action of God, it is not only a false but also a *dangerous* view for us to hold (Rom 1:19–20; CCC 287). It implies that humans are mere animals. And, as the 20th Century showed, it is only a very short step from saying human beings are animals to treating them that way.

Here are some guidelines on what a Catholic should believe regarding creation and evolution.

The first three chapters of Genesis "pertain to history in a true sense even though the inspired author may have used a poetic literary form to communicate these truths" (CCC 289; *Humani Generis*). When the Church says "pertain to history in a true sense," it means something that really happened. The first sin (original sin, the fall of our first parents) really happened at a certain time and place in history. Perhaps it was six thousand years ago; perhaps six hundred thousand years ago. For all we know, the first sin may well have had something to do with eating a certain fruit that God had commanded man not to eat. But it need not have. That may simply be a poetic way the Genesis writer chose to communicate the historical truth about man's fall from paradise. What we must affirm is that there really was a first sin (Rom 5:12; CCC 390, 396, 397).

We must also affirm the following:

1. All things were created by a loving God (Jn 1:1–3; CCC 291, 315).

2. Man is made in the image of God, which means, among other things, that he is a spiritual being with the powers of knowing and freely choosing (Gn 1:27; CCC 355).

3. Even if man's body evolved, God still created man, because God created the process of evolution, and His providence guided it to give rise to the human race (Jn 1:3; CCC 302, 308).

4. Whatever the origin of man's bodily form, his soul is a special creation of God; it is not the result of an evolutionary process (Gn 2:7; CCC 362-367). This is because spirit, unlike matter, is incapable of evolving, since it has no parts that could evolve from one thing to another. The soul is the direct creation of God, not a product of matter.

5. Our original parents were created in a state of perfect happiness, a state of "holiness and justice" (Gn 2:7–9; CCC 375, 376, 398).

6. Their obedience was tested and they transgressed the divine law at the prompting of the devil (Gn 3:1–7; CCC 397).

7. They lost the supernatural gifts given to the human race by God at creation (Gn 3:16–19; CCC 400). (For example, freedom from bodily death, freedom from suffering, perfect control of the soul over the body).

8. This state of original sin was passed on to their offspring. (Rom 5:12–19; CCC 402). Therefore, all human beings are born in this wounded and weakened condition (CCC 404).

9. They were promised a redeemer (Gn 3:15; CCC 410), who would restore mankind's relationship with God.

As long as these basic elements of Catholic teaching on creation are held, Catholics may accept the theory of evolution. Nevertheless, a Catholic is not obliged to do so if he or she thinks the evidence is against it. Evolution is a scientific theory, not a theological dogma. It stands or falls on the evidence.

Question #20

"It seems to me that you have to believe that either evolution or creation is true. How can you believe both at the same time, as I hear some people say?" Alice B., 15

A. By holding that God used evolution as His way of forming human beings. In that sense, you could say the *only* way a Catholic can believe in evolution is *also* to believe in creation. Now, the opposite is not true; you can believe in creation without affirming evolution.

When some people (usually fundamentalist Protestants and atheists) place evolution and creation in opposition, they usually mean evolution by blind chance vs. creation in the sense of God literally fashioning man from "the dust of the earth" and "breathing" into him the "breath of life" all in six twenty-four-hour days. Obviously, creation and evolution in those senses cannot both be true. People think there is a conflict between creation and evolution because they think the only alternatives are the strict fundamentalist view and the atheistic materialist view. Fundamentalists insist the creation story in Genesis must be interpreted as strict history in every detail. For them, it is not enough to say the creation and fall of man really happened; they insist it must have happened according to their literalistic reading of the Genesis narrative, without considering that parts of it may be poetic or allegorical. Atheistic materialists, on the other hand, say the creation of the human race (and the universe as a whole) was due to blind chance, without any divine intervention, whether by evolution or any other means.

This is a false set of choices. If evolution is understood as a process designed by God, and creation as simply God's act of bringing everything into existence in some way, then there need not be a conflict. The answer does not need to be either evolution or creation; it can be both evolution and creation.

A Catholic may completely embrace the creation narrative as a historical depiction in every detail, but he is not required by the Church to do so, and he may not condemn other Catholics who do not agree with him. He may also embrace evolutionary theory as a scientific explanation, as long as he doesn't deny the fundamental Christian truths mentioned in the previous question.

Question #21

"If we were created by God, why do scientists have such strong evidence that we evolved from apes?" Jennie F., 17

A. There is disagreement about just how strong such evidence is and about the meaning of this evidence. Because evolution has been taught as fact for the past several decades in our schools, most people accept it as true. They do not know about the problems with the theory, nor that the evidence can be interpreted in a number of ways.

Evolutionary science is not the stable discipline we are led to believe. It involves a lot of self-correction and revision. For example, theories about the variations of early man used to divide early man into different types, including Peking man, Java man, and Neanderthal man. Today, they are all considered one—*homo erectus*. Scientists now see that different fossils (of which there are few) are essentially the same. (For more information, see the secular website www.modernhumanorigins.com—a brief summary of this issue is presented.)

Theories that early man was ferocious are now being refuted. Evidence shows that early man was quite advanced in the development and use of tools. He performed amputations and even buried the deceased with flowers. These are not acts of a beast. In addition, these issues point to the central problem: what makes a human being human is not opposable thumbs, nor even the ability to make tools (chimps can do that). It is the existence of a rational soul. And that is not something fossils can show us.

Other problems exist too. Some scientists are too eager to speak beyond the evidence they possess, just as some fundamentalists are too eager to find dinosaurs mentioned in Scripture. For instance, in 1911, French anatomist Marcellin Boule's Neanderthal skeleton led him to conclude that early man was hunched over with his face thrust forward, similar to the gorilla (see a summary of Boule's views at anthro.palomar. edu/homo2/neandertal.htm). Forty-five years later, a team of anatomists re-examined Boule's skeleton and concluded the hunched over stance was not due to genetics but to severe arthritis.

Because evolutionary scientists (unlike chemists and physicists) are unable to test their hypotheses in a controlled laboratory, their theories are developed from "reasonable interpretations" and even imagination. Fossil evidence needs to be interpreted; it does not speak for itself.

Based on developments from the 1970s to the present, evolution, especially Darwin's theory of natural selection, is being called into serious question by respected scientists. The theory may still be true, but opposing opinions, which were blocked out of academic life because of materialist prejudice and antireligious sentiment, are now being heard. If you're interested in learning more, I recommend reading *Darwin on Trial* by Phillip Johnson or Michael Behe's *Darwin's Black Box*. Both are listed in the Resources section at the end of this book. (Also recommended: the *Adam, Eve, and Evolution* article on the Catholic Answers' website www.catholic.com).

This is not to say that evolutionary theory is necessarily false. Pope John Paul II, in a 1996 address to the Pontifical Academy of the Sciences, made it clear that new knowledge has led to the recognition of the theory of evolution as more than a hypothesis. In short, there are many pieces of evidence, from a lot of scientific disciplines, pointing to the high probability of human descent from a common ancestor.

The bottom line: We will never know the full story of how the human race came into existence, though we may discover a few material fragments of evidence about how our bodies were created. We can learn the spiritual side of our early history from the only infallible, irrefutable source: God, speaking through the Scriptures and the Church.

Chapter 3

RELIGION AND THE BIBLE

Question #22

"How did we get the Bible?" Ryan C., 16

A. There are two answers to your question: one from history, the other from theology.

We do not have space here to go into great detail about the history of the Bible. Suffice it to say that the Bible as we know it today was composed over a period of almost a thousand years. The Old Testament books were written mainly in Hebrew (with a bit of Aramaic and some Greek), the New Testament entirely in Greek. They were copied by hand and preserved with remarkable accuracy, as archeological findings such as the Dead Sea Scrolls confirm.

The theological answer to your question is easier to state: God inspired the biblical writers to write the Bible we have today (2 Tm 3:16; 2 Pt 1:19-21; CCC 105, 136). This means that, without revoking their freedom, God so moved them that they wrote what He wanted them to write. In this sense, God is the primary Author of the Bible; the human authors remained true authors as well, using their own particular gifts and abilities to convey without error those truths that God wanted to teach us (CCC 106). This is the doctrine of biblical inspiration—

the Bible is the Word of God without ceasing also to be the words of men (CCC 105, 702).

You may want to look at some short books that trace the Bible's history. The first is *Where We Got the Bible* (Catholic Answers). The second is a short booklet, *How the Bible Has Come to Us* (Scepter Press). Lastly, *The Catholic Church and the Bible* (Ignatius Press) is an excellent resource as well.

Question #23

"How do we know the Bible is the written Word of God?" Thang P., 19

A. We know the Bible is inspired because the Catholic Church has constantly taught that it is, and we have Jesus' promise that He won't allow the Church to err on such a basic issue (Mt 16:18–19; CCC 136). Indeed, we see that Jesus himself spoke of Scriptures as the inspired word of God, which bore witness to him (Lk 24:44-47). But, someone might ask, how do we know, apart from the Bible, that Jesus promised He would preserve the Church from erring on such things? And if we have to rely on the Bible to know that, isn't this circular reasoning: using the Bible to support the Church and the Church to justify the Bible?

No, it isn't a circular argument to rely on the Bible here but a "spiral" one. Let me explain: Let's start with the Bible as a merely human record (the general reliability of which we can defend on historical grounds without appealing to revelation) to show who Jesus is—the Son of God (Mt 3:16–17; Jn 3:16; CCC 444). (The argument for Christ's divinity we have to assume for the moment.)

Then we show that Jesus told His followers that He would guide them and that He chose apostles to do so after His ascension (Lk 6:13–16). In other words, He established a teaching authority in the Church and endowed it with His special guidance (Mt 16:18–19, 18:15–18; Jn 14:25–26; CCC 889, 892). Again, at this point, we are using the Bible as a mere human record of what happened, not as the inspired Word of God.

Next, we show that the Church Christ promised to guide has declared certain writings to be inspired. The list of inspired books that the Church put together is called the Canon of Scripture (CCC 120). ("Canon" with one "n," which means a standard of measure, not a military weapon.)

Because Christ is the Son of God, when He promises something, He has the power to make sure it happens (Heb 1:3). He promised to guide His followers and to do it through the apostles (Jn 14:16–18, 25–26). The apostles in turn passed along a share in their authority to the bishops (Ti 1:5–9), who later officially declared the biblical books to be inspired. Their declaration did not, of course, *make* the Bible inspired; God did that when He moved men to write the various books. What the Church did was to settle once and for all which books are divinely inspired. And she did it with the authority of Christ who had promised to be with her (Mt 28:20; CCC 860).

This argument is based on faith that Christ is Who He claimed to be and that He will do as He promised (Heb 10:23). Believing these things is not blind faith (that is, faith opposed to reason or without reason).

True, we can't fully "see" from reason alone that Christ is the Son of God, but this does not make faith in such things unreasonable. True faith is supra-rational (above reason), not irrational (against reason). In fact, it is the alternative explanations of Jesus' identity (that he was a Nice Guy, a Liar, a Lunatic, or a Guru) that require blind faith.

There is another approach to the Bible's inspiration we can take. We can show how certain things are best explained on the premise that the Bible is the inspired, written Word of God. For example, we can look at the fulfillment of biblical prophecy (Mt 2:6, 4:14–16; Is 53; CCC 128). Does this not suggest that the Scripture has a more than human origin (2 Pt 1:19–21)? Of course, this approach doesn't *absolutely* prove the inspiration of the Bible, but it does strongly support the idea (CCC 135).

Question #24

"What is the difference between the Old and New Testaments?" Alyssa W., 14

A. The Old Testament is the collection of books that record the story of creation; the fall of man through sin; the call of Abraham; the Exodus from Egypt and the covenant with Israel; the giving of the Law (including the Ten Commandments) and the entry into the Holy Land; the establishment of David's kingdom; the promise of God given through the prophets of a messiah (Jesus); the life and trials of the chosen people, the Jews, as they struggled to be faithful while waiting for the Messiah; and the events leading up to Jesus' coming (CCC 122).

The Old Testament contains forty-six books which are traditionally divided into four categories: the Pentateuch (also called the Torah or the Law), the historical books, the wisdom books, and the prophetic books. A list of the books in each of these categories can usually be found in the instructional pages of your Bible (CCC 120, 138).

The New Testament begins with the birth of Jesus, but it tells us little about the life of Christ before He began His public ministry around the age of thirty. It recounts the ministry, passion, death, resurrection, and ascension of Jesus, as well as the story of the early Church, and it offers a rich collection of early letters from various figures in the early Church on the meaning of Christ for us.

The New Testament can also be divided into four kinds of writing: the Gospels, summaries of Jesus' life and teaching; the letters (also called *epistles*) of various apostles and apostolic men (Paul, Peter, James, John, Jude and the author of Hebrews) to early Catholic communities and individuals; the Acts of the Apostles, a history of the early Christians; and the Apocalypse (or Revelation). There are twenty-seven books in the New Testament (CCC 120, 124).

In short, the Old Testament is the story of the Jewish people, and the New Testament is the story of the Catholic people, both Jews and Gentiles (non-Jews), who accepted and followed Christ.

Question #25

"Are the stories in the Bible true?" Stephen C., 15

A. Yes, all the stories in the Bible are true, but not all are intended to be read as history. The parables of Jesus contain life-changing truths that can lead us to a deeper understanding of God and His message of repentance, love, and truth. But that does not mean things described in the parables necessarily really happened (Lk 8:9–10). We do not have to think there really was a Prodigal Son, for example (Lk 15:11–32). Jesus used this story to illustrate the love of the Father for us.

On the other hand, when the biblical author intended to say that something really did happen, then it really did happen. The Gospel writers intended to say that Jesus Christ really lived, suffered, died, and rose from the dead. That is not a parable, and they did not intend it to be viewed as one (1 Cor 15:14; CCC 137).

This requires a bit of common sense. Many think the Bible is one big fat book written in only one way. It is not. There are many different writers using several different styles or "genres" of writing. We see this in our own experience. The news anchor on CNN is telling the truth (we hope) in a different way than a play by Shakespeare or a song by a poet or a sermon by a saint. Their "styles" are different and the way they speak the truth is different. You do not expect Shakespeare to deliver the truth via a stock market quote, and you do not expect the anchorman to burst into a sonnet to deliver the weather report. But both speak the truth in their own ways.

The same with the Scriptures. The Bible sometimes aims to give a historical chronicle of real events that really occurred. At other times it employs poetry, myth, or fiction, in order to convey truth according to that genre. Nobody thinks Jesus "lied" because there wasn't really a Prodigal Son. Likewise, nobody thinks that because Jesus used parables or stories to teach a moral truth, it must therefore follow that nothing in the Bible is historical.

Whether a given story is history, then, depends on the intent of the author in telling it. How do we know what the writer intended? That requires properly interpreting the Bible in accordance with the Tradition of the Church. It is the responsibility of the Magisterium (that is, the pope and the bishops), with the assistance of trained biblical scholars, to guide us in this matter.

Question #26

"What does the Bible have to offer the world today?" Nathan T., 15

A. The Bible offers the living Word of God to all people in all ages (2 Tm 3:16–17). That living Word is Christ Himself (Jn 1:1; CCC 101-103, 461).

Christ fully reveals us to ourselves. He shows us why we are here and where we are headed (Ps 119:105). Through Jesus we can know the meaning and purpose of life (Jn 17:3).

The Bible brings Christ to us (2 Tm 3:15). The truth of Christ presented in the Bible can remedy the world's ills and bring us to everlasting happiness with God and peace with ourselves (Rom 5:1).

Question #27

"Why is religion so important in our lives?" Jeff H., 14

A. It depends on what you mean by "religion." Not all religions are true or equally true, so religion as such is not really the issue. If by "religion" you mean the truths about God and man's relation to Him, that is important simply because it is true. It is the way things are. So the Catholic faith is important because it is true and helps us to know the Ultimate Reality, God.

Our religion is also important because it helps us fulfill our purpose, to become the human beings God most deeply desires we beome, both as individuals and as a society (CCC 2105). God made us for a purpose, and unless we consult what He has revealed about that purpose and live accordingly, we will be failed creatures, as useless as a screen door on a submarine or a bathing suit in a snowstorm (2 Cor 5:1–5; Sir 17:1–13; Is 43:21).

Because the Catholic faith reveals why we are here, it shows us the meaning of life. It can keep us from despair and prepare us for the fulfillment of our existence in the next life (Phil 4:4–7; Rom 15:13). It also provides guidelines for human society (Rom 3:19–20). Imagine what things would be like without the moral laws and principles true religion provides. Everyone would do what he or she selfishly liked without any regard for others. This would lead to complete self-indulgence, which leads to all types of vice and sin (Rom 1:18–32; CCC 57, 401). True religious belief teaches us to get out of ourselves and turn to God and others (Mt 22:35–40).

Question #28

"Why are religion and church so boring?"
Colin M., 16

A. There are no boring things, only bored people. If God made all things and, subsequently, knows the meaning of all things, how could the study of God possibly be boring? We sometimes make our faith boring, but it is not boring when properly taught and seriously studied.

Sometimes we are addicted to superficial kinds of excitement—that is one drawback of too much television and its never-ending stimulation in our lives. When it comes to really important things like God, the reasons for our existence, and what lies ahead of us after death, we yawn and flip to the next TV channel. It is not that God is boring. Rather, He is too much for us. We tune Him out because He challenges us.

But sooner or later, the realities of life catch up with us, and we are forced to face the "RBQs"—Really Big Questions. Then we see that religion and church are anything but boring, because they help us answer these questions.

Chapter 4

JESUS CHRIST

Question #29

"Is Jesus God or is He God's Son?" Melissa D., 15

A. He is both. To say Jesus is God means that He is a divine person, the Second Person of the Trinity, and that He possesses the divine nature: He acts as God acts (Jn 1:1, 20:28; Col. 1:15 2:9; CCC 240, 242). To say He is the Son of God means that He is the Son of the Father, the First Person of the Trinity, and that He possesses the same divine nature as the Father (Mt 3:16–17; Heb 1:1–3; CCC 262).

Perhaps this analogy will help: As a human being, you are the child of human parents, not mere animal parents. You possess a human nature from them. Well, Jesus is the eternal Son of the Father. He existed from all eternity with the Father as the divine Son before assuming a human nature and being born in Bethlehem two thousand years ago. He has existed from all eternity with the Father, eternally proceeding from Him as light streams forth from the sun (Jn 1:1–5). And as you share a common human nature with your parents, so the Son shares the divine nature with God the Father (and the Holy Spirit) (Heb 1:3; Col 2:9). In that sense, we can speak of Jesus as the Son of God, because He is God the Son, the Second Person of the Trinity.

There is, however, another sense in which Jesus is the Son of God. Jesus Christ possesses two natures, a human nature and a divine nature (CCC 423, 430). Jesus is also the Son of God in the sense that God alone is the Father of His human nature. The doctrine of the virginal conception and birth holds that Jesus had no earthly father (Mt 1:18–23; Lk 1:26–38).

Another thing to keep in mind is that Jesus is not 50 percent human and 50 percent divine. He is 100 percent human and 100 percent divine (1 Tm 2:5). This joining of the two natures is called the Hypostatic Union (CCC 252, 464, 470).

Question #30
"How do we know Jesus even existed?" Dave G., 14

A. How do we know George Washington or Abraham Lincoln ever existed? We were not there. We rely on history and records from that period. So. too, with Christ.

The primary record of His existence is the Bible. Although we Christians usually think of the Bible as the Word of God, we should remember that much of it is a historical record as well (CCC 126). The New Testament documents, in particular, give us vital historical information about Jesus, even though they are not intended to be extensive biographies in the modern sense.

The New Testament picture of Jesus is supported by non-Christian historical sources, although there are not many of these that have survived from the time of the early Church. The probable reason for such scant non-Christian historical evidence is that the Romans, who were the main historians of the time, would not have been concerned with a small outpost of their empire like Palestine. The Jewish historian Josephus does record the existence of Jesus and the fact that He was executed under Pontius Pilate. This supports the New Testament account, as do all other ancient secular references to Christ, such as those found in the works of the Roman writers Tacitus, Suetonius, and Pliny the Younger. In fact, no serious historian today doubts that Jesus existed.

Question #31

"Why was Jesus killed on the cross?" Steven O., 13

A. Because many Jewish priests and elders at that time, as well as pagan Roman leaders, were greatly disturbed and threatened by His message (Mk 7:1–13; Jn 2:12–16). The Jewish leaders saw Him as a threat to the Jewish law (Lk 22:66–71; Jn 18:19–19:7). The Roman leaders were concerned that He would cause a political uprising (Jn 19:12–16; Lk 23:1–24; 1 Cor 15:3; CCC 601, 619).

Question #32

"Why does Jesus love us so much?" Clare M., 16

A. Because He is God (Jn 1:1, 20:28). God loves us perfectly (1 Jn 4:8). Our finite minds are unable to grasp the infinite (Job 11:7–9). This is why we will never fully understand why God loves us so much.

The first and most basic way we know Jesus loves us is that He made us (Jn 1:1–3). This is an act of love (CCC

291, 315). But even more than making us, He loves us even after we have sinned against Him and rejected Him. The evidence of Jesus' love for us is that He died for our sins. Scripture says: "No one has greater love than this, to lay down one's life for one's friends" (Jn 15:13; CCC 609). Jesus' death for us on the cross was the supreme act of love (Jn 3:16; CCC 219, 458).

Question #33

"Is there any record of how Jesus was in His younger years, ages ten to twelve or so?"
Charity W., 17

A. The only thing we know of Jesus' younger years is that, at age twelve, He was found by His parents in the temple discussing matters with the priests and elders (Lk 2:41–51; CCC 534). Upon finding Jesus, His parents asked, "Son, why have You done this to us? Your father and I have been looking for You with great anxiety" (Lk 2:48). To which Jesus responded, "Why were you looking for Me? Did you not know that I must be in My Father's house" (Lk 2:49; CCC 583)? Jesus then left with His parents and was obedient to them (Lk 2:51; CCC 531). The fact that the God-Man would be obedient to His parents offers us a valuable lesson.

There are claims of private revelations about Jesus' early years, but Catholics are not required to accept them. Private revelations must be distinguished from the *public* revelation of God revealed in the Bible and in the Sacred Tradition of the Church. This public revelation—that is, Church teaching—we *are* required to believe. Also, we should always be cautious about private revelations because they may include serious errors about Christ.

Question #34

"Assuming Jesus was God, is He responsible for all things? For example, did Jesus build my hot rod?" Matthew S., 16

A.Your fellow teenagers may know that this question is actually the title of a pop song (and therefore probably not a serious question), but I want to answer it anyhow. There are some great theological truths we can learn if we take it seriously.

The short answer is "No, a mechanic built it," but Jesus "built" the mechanic. He also built the physical universe upon which mechanics rely. It was He who said that gasoline should undergo combustion and that the metal in your car should behave like metal and not like wood or water. In short, all creation comes from God, and Jesus is God, so all creation *ultimately* comes from Jesus (Jn 1:1–3; Col 1:15–16; CCC 292).

At the root of your question is the notion that something can have only one cause. But this is not so. A thing can have more than one cause. God is the First Cause of everything. But a human being can be a secondary— and real—cause of something.

God made the matter out of which your car was made (2 Mc 7:28). He made the man who made the car. He gave that man the intellect and freedom to acquire the skill to make your car. God permitted the circumstances in which the man used his skills to make your car. So, the First Cause of the car is God, but the man who built the car is a secondary and real cause. And, of course, God keeps your hot rod in existence, moment by moment

(Col 1:17; Heb 1:3; CCC 291, 301). Let us not claim more for your car than that.

Chapter 5

THE CATHOLIC FAITH
AND THE CHURCH

Question #35

"Why be a Catholic?" Justin M., 15

A. Being a Catholic is how you fulfill the purpose of your existence: to know God and to be united with Him (Jn 15:1–7; CCC 737). The means that God has given us to enter that relationship with Him is faith in and obedience to His Son, Jesus (Jn 14:15). This obedience includes following Jesus' commands, including being baptized (Jn 3:3–5; CCC 782) which makes you a part of his Body, the Church.

The way we know and love Jesus is through His Church, which He established to teach, sanctify, and shepherd people in His name (Mt 16:16–19; Lk 10:16; Eph 4:11–12; CCC 552, 794, 869). That means He wants you to belong to the Catholic Church. Why else would He go to the trouble of establishing it?

Through the teaching of the Church, Christ gives us His truth infallibly, which means it is handed on to us without error (Mt 16:19, 18:18; 1 Tm 3:15; CCC 171, 553). Through the sacraments and prayer of the Church, Christ gives us His grace and sanctifies us (Eph 4:7; 1 Cor 6:11; CCC 913, 1695, 2813). Through the pastoral authority of the Church, Christ governs and shepherds us as His people (1 Pt 5:1–4; CCC 893, 1551).

By the way, the word *catholic* is from the Greek word *katholikos,* meaning "universal." This is the Church you belong to, the "universal" Church. This means that the gospel of truth Jesus entrusted to his Church is to be preached to all people throughout the entire world, to people of every nation, race, and time. The Church is to exist everywhere (CCC 831).

Question #36

"Can you give a brief history of our faith?"
Erin O., 15

A. Jesus was the Messiah for whom the Jews were waiting (Mt 16:16). Approximately two thousand years ago He was born of a virgin (Mt 1:18–25). Around age 33, He was unjustly put to death (Mk 15:24–37). Three days later, Jesus rose from the dead. Forty days after that Jesus ascended into heaven, and then sent the Holy Spirit to empower His apostles to spread His gospel. He established the Catholic Church on Peter, the first pope, whom Jesus called the "rock" (Mt 16:18; CCC 552, 881).

The Church started out small in Jerusalem but grew as people saw the wonderful changes in their lives and the heroic martyrdoms of some of the first Catholics. In a remarkably short time, it had spread throughout the Roman Empire and beyond. Around the year 313, Constantine decreed that Christianity could be legally practiced. Around the year 390, the Church established the final version of the Bible. Over the first thousand years of the Church's history there were many false teachings (called *heresies*) and questions that sprouted up. These forced the Church to define and clarify its doctrines.

In the year 1054, a formal split occurred between the Eastern and Western Catholic Churches. The Eastern Church is still separated from us. It is referred to as the Eastern Orthodox Church, of which there are many national churches (for example, Greek Orthodox, Russian Orthodox, and Romanian Orthodox). Though the Eastern Orthodox accept most Catholic beliefs, they do not accept the authority of the pope.

One of the most devastating events in Christian history occurred in the year 1517 at the hands of a monk named Martin Luther. In his attempt to correct some of the abuses in the Church (and some would say to address his psychological problem of scrupulosity), he broke away from the Church and established a new system of theology. He promoted a new doctrine called *sola scriptura* ("the Scripture alone") which basically holds that the ultimate authority for Christians is the Bible alone, not a teaching Church. Luther held that we do not need a teaching Church to guide us to Christian truth. One simply needs to interpret the Bible on his own to find out what is and is not true. This new doctrine has led to chaos. Today there are hundreds (if not thousands) of Protestant denominations, most of which were formed due to disagreements over key points of Christian belief and practice. This is a fruit of the man-made tradition of "private interpretation."

From the 1500s until the present, the Church has continued to grow. It has nourished many of the institutions and disciplines we have today, including art, music, medicine, law, farming, architecture, formalized schooling, literature, and more. In fact, many historians would admit that the Catholic Church is clearly the most influential organization in the history of the world.

Naturally, there is much more. The life of the Church is more intriguing than any soap opera or novel you could read. It has saints and sinners. It has been heroic and cowardly. But despite any human failings, the Church is still the bride of Christ (Eph 5:21–32; CCC 796, 808). And, if anything is standing at the end of time, it will be the Church because it alone has been given the gifts of infallibility, indefectibility, and indestructibility (Mt 16:18–19, 28:20; CCC 553, 788, 889).

For a good short book on the Church's history, I recommend *A Short History of the Catholic Church* by Jose Orlandis or *Triumph* by Harry Crocker. Both are listed in the Resources section.

Question #37

"How do you prove that the Catholic faith is the 'correct' religion to believe in?" Jennie F., 17

A. First, you have to ask whether Jesus is God and the Messiah the world was waiting for. You then need to find out which Church is the one true Church He established. To do this, you should look for the Church that has all the aspects of the Church identified in Scripture.

Let us first address the question of whether Jesus was God. When considering this question, we can only conclude one of four things: 1) He was a liar, 2) He was a lunatic, 3) He was a guru, or 4) He was Lord. Let me try to succinctly point out that He had to be God and Lord.

To begin, Jesus clearly indicated that He was God and accepted the worship due God in several places in Scripture (see, for instance, Jn 8:58; 20:26-29). He performed dozens of recorded miracles to substantiate His claim, including walking on water (Mt 14:25), feeding the five-thousand with just five loaves of bread and two fish (Mk 6:34–44), and raising people from the dead (Mt 9:18–26; Jn 11:1–44).

In addition, ten of the twelve apostles died as martyrs for this belief in Jesus (Judas betrayed Jesus and hanged himself, and the apostle John died a natural death). The ten apostles who chose to be killed would not have done this had they not believed He was the Messiah or seen Him prove His divinity by His miracles.

Jesus cannot be a liar. He chose to die a brutal death and turned down offers of political power. A liar (or opportunist) would do neither.

Jesus cannot be a lunatic or "crazy." His teachings were rational and His thinking was calculated and very clear.

Jesus cannot be a "guru" (that is, a "New Age master") trying to "raise our consciousness" and tell us we are all God. He flatly denied that we are all God. He made it very clear that He was without sin and we are not. He is from above, we are from below (Jn 8:1-11, 8:23).

So, it becomes very difficult to come up with an explanation other than Peter's: "You are the Christ, the Son of the Living God" (Mt 16:16). Assuming then that Jesus was God, we need to look for what He came to do. Scripture reveals that He came to die for our sins (1 Tm

2:5–6; Heb 2:17) and establish a Church that would teach in His name when He went to heaven (Mt 16:18; 18:17; 1 Tm 3:15).

To find the true Church established by Christ, we need to look at Scripture and history. All Catholic doctrines are either explicitly or implicitly supported by Scripture (CCC 86). Nothing the Church teaches, when properly understood, goes against Scripture or reason. Furthermore, only the Catholic Church fits completely the pattern of the Church in the New Testament. Only the Catholic Church is visibly one in faith, in sacraments, and in church government with the successor of St. Peter, the pope.

A strong case for the Catholic faith is also made by studying history. If you look at the extra-biblical writings of the early Christians, you will see that they taught Catholic doctrines. In fact, the Roman Catholic Church was often referred to by name. The first recorded usage of the word *catholic* is found as early as 107 AD. A disciple of the apostle John, St. Ignatius of Antioch, said: "Wherever the bishop appears, let the people be there, just as wherever Jesus Christ is, there is the catholic church" (*Epistle to the Smyrnaeans, 8:2*).

The Catholic Church can trace its authority as the one true Church through its unbroken line of more than 260 popes from John Paul II back to St. Peter. All other Christian churches are offshoots of the Catholic Church. These churches were founded by mere men or women, not by Jesus, who was God in the flesh.

Question #38

"Is the Catholic religion the only correct religion?"
Beth R., 14

A. All religions contain some truth (CCC 843). Some religions contain more truth than others. For example, Protestant Christianity is much closer to the truth than Mormonism, because Protestants believe there is one God, whereas Mormonism incorrectly teaches there are many gods (CCC 2112).

Eastern Orthodoxy contains more truth than Protestantism because, in addition to the basic Christian beliefs such as the divinity of Jesus and the Virgin Birth, it affirms Jesus' real presence in the Eucharist, honors the saints who have died before us, possesses a valid apostolic succession from the apostles in its bishops, and affirms many other Catholic beliefs. It does not, however, accept the authority of the pope.

The Catholic Church says that, although other faiths contain truth, the fullness of what God has revealed to the world *subsists* (that is, concretely and essentially exists) in the Catholic Church. Other religions or faiths are correct to the extent that they hold the revealed truths given to the apostles and passed on to the present-day bishops in the Catholic Church.

This does **not** mean that only those who are visible members of the Catholic Church can be saved (Acts 10:34–35; Rom 2:14–16). God can save whomever He desires and has surely done so outside the visible structure of the Catholic Church (Lk 9:49–50; CCC 169). However, the surest means to salvation is found in the

Catholic Church. Its doctrines are the ones infallibly given by Jesus (Mt 16:19, 18:18; 1 Tm 3:15; CCC 889).

Here is an analogy to illustrate this point: Let's imagine that you want to travel from city "A" to city "B." Everyone in the area knows that Highway 7 is the best route. Why? Because it has all the things necessary for a safe trip: gas stations to buy fuel for your car, rest stops where you can get some food to eat, auto repair service in case your car breaks down, and signs that tell you which way to go.

Well, the Church is like Highway 7: it is the best route to get from here to heaven. It has spiritual "gas stations"— the sacraments—where you can fill up your soul with "spiritual fuel" (that is, grace). It has "rest stops" (i.e., churches) where you can receive your "spiritual food"— the Holy Eucharist. It has a "spiritual repair service" for when your soul "breaks down" in sin—confession. And it has all the necessary signs to guide you to your ultimate destination (i.e., heaven)—the Scriptures, Sacred Tradition, and the Magisterium. Without these aids we may be saved, but it will certainly be more difficult. (Remember: This is an analogy and, like any analogy, is imperfect. It does, however, communicate the basic truth about the Catholic faith.)

Question #39

"Why is the Catholic Church so closed-minded?"
Ellie M., 17

A. As Catholic apologist G.K. Chesterton said, the purpose of an open mind, like that of an open mouth, is to close it on something solid (see his book *Orthodoxy*). For the mind, that "something solid" is truth. When we do not know the truth but seek it, we are free to be (in fact, we should be) open-minded. But once we have come to a firm conviction of the truth of something, to remain "open-minded" about it is foolishness. Most people are not "open-minded" about whether murder is good or theft bad. They have made up their minds and rightly so.

When it comes to religious issues, the Catholic Church has "made up its mind" on a certain body of truths. There are good reasons for what the Church teaches, so it is not a matter of "closed-mindedness" in the wrong sense. It is a question of reasoned conviction.

This is not to say that the Catholic Church is dogmatic about everything. In fact, the remarkable thing about the Church is how much "gray area" it leaves us. The Church is like a human body. It has a certain number of dogmatic "bones" that are hard and unbending. But the purpose of those bones is to make the body of Christ flexible and able to move and think in a huge number of very creative ways.

Another important point to remember: The Catholic faith comes from God (Lk 10:16; 1 Tm 3:15; CCC 87, 858). When God has definitely said something in the Scriptures or Sacred Tradition, neither the pope nor the bishops, nor the priests and deacons are free to change Catholic doctrines to appear "open-minded" (Acts 20:28). Their job is simply to tell people the truth in a loving manner (Jn 8:31–32; Gal 4:16). They do not make up or determine the truth for themselves (2 Cor 13:8).

A final note: Being too "open-minded" can be hazardous to your spiritual and physical health. You may fall for every radical new idea that comes along, or allow yourself to be swept away by the latest diet fads or consumer trends. As a priest friend of mine once remarked, "Some people's minds are so open, they ought to be closed for repairs." Fortunately, the Church can help such people make these "repairs" by guiding them in the truth.

Question #40

"How does one become a Catholic?" Jennifer F., 17

A. I assume you mean teenagers or adults, not babies.

First, a person studies the faith. Then if he or she chooses to embrace it, he or she will make a formal profession of faith, accepting what the Church teaches as true. Next, the person will be baptized if he or she has not been already (Acts 8:36–38, 18:8; CCC 1252, 1654). Usually the new convert will also receive the other sacraments of initiation, confirmation and Holy Eucharist, at this time (Acts 2:41–42; 8:14–17; CCC 1226). Those already validly baptized make a profession of faith and then receive the sacraments of confirmation, reconciliation, and the Holy Eucharist (CCC 1315).

If you are interested in becoming a Catholic, you should contact the local parish to find out what steps need to be taken. I also recommend reading a good book like the late Fr. John Hardon's *The Faith*, which is an instruction book based on the new *Catechism*, to help supplement the education you will receive at the parish. This book is listed in the Resources section.

Chapter 6

THE CATHOLIC FAITH AND OTHER RELIGIONS

Question #41

"If you get confirmed, could you join another faith, such as Baha'i, later on?" Alice B., 15

A. Confirmation is a statement that you freely choose to be a "soldier for Christ" and the Catholic Church. A real soldier would not fight for both sides (Mk 3:24–25). You cannot simultaneously profess one faith and then another without violating the laws of logic. Different faiths teach different things or they would be together. Basic logic says that if one group says that "X" is true and another says that "X" is false, they both cannot be right.

Regarding Baha'i specifically, it was founded by Mirza Husayn 'Ali Huri, who took another name that means "Glory of God." One of the central tenets of this religion is the "common foundation of all religion." This sounds nice but is an impossibility because of the fundamental differences among religions. Who determines what "common foundation" means? Is that person or group of people infallible? If not, how can we trust their teachings?

There have been thousands of new faiths that have popped up over the past four hundred years, especially in the last hundred years. In time Baha'i, like most of the others, will fall by the wayside. Only the Catholic Church is founded by God Himself (Mt 16:18; CCC 424) and its teachings will be guided and protected until the end of time (Mt 28:19–20; CCC 860) because it is the only religion established by the God-Man Himself, Jesus Christ.

Question #42

"If you leave the Catholic faith for another faith, can you come back to the Church if you do not like the other religion?" Travis G., 15

A. Yes, and you can bet the angels in heaven will be rejoicing when you do (Lk 15:10; CCC 545).

Remember the story of the Prodigal Son? He came back to his father after living a wild life and spending his inheritance. When his father saw him in the distance, he ran to meet him, threw his arms around him, and gave a great feast to celebrate his return (Lk 15:11–32; CCC 1439). This is surely the way God feels when someone returns to the Catholic faith. But of course, it is better if you do not leave at all.

Question #43

"Isn't any religion the right one depending on the culture from which you come?" Emily F., 15

A. No. God's truth transcends cultures and time (Jn 18:37). His truth is the same in every place and every age (Ps 119:89–90; Jn 14:6; CCC 74, 459, 2466).

If religious truth were culturally relative, we would have to accept the human sacrifices of the Aztecs because that sort of thing was acceptable to Aztec culture. This, of course, would not be good. If God reveals a truth, it is true in all places for all time.

Question #44

"What's the difference between Catholic and Christian?" Jonathan S., 14

A. Nothing. To be Catholic is to be fully Christian. However, often when people ask this question, what they really mean, without being able to articulate it clearly, is "What is the difference between the Catholic faith and Protestant Christianity?"

All Catholics are Christians, but not all Christians are Catholics. A Christian is someone who believes in Jesus Christ as the Son of God and is baptized. A Catholic is a specific kind of Christian—one who also believes the Catholic Church was founded by Christ and accepts it as possessing the fullness of Christian truth and the means of salvation (Mt 16:18–19; 1 Tm 3:15; CCC 2032, 2033, 2051).

Being Catholic involves three main things: (1) sincerely holding to the Catholic faith as taught by the Magisterium, which is the official teaching body of the Church (2 Thess 2:15; CCC 1113, 1129); (2) accepting the sacraments of the Catholic Church; and (3) submitting to the teaching authority of the pope and the bishops in communion with him (1 Thess 5:12–13; CCC 1269).

The words *Catholic* and *Christian* were once interchangeable. The first Christians called the Church "Catholic" or "universal," to distinguish it from heretical splinter groups that denied necessary Christian truths.

Thus the early Christians came to be known as Catholics.

Around the year 1,000 AD, many Christians in the East—in Greece and in what is now Turkey—split off from the Catholic Church. They are called Orthodox Christians. They believe many of the same things we do, but they reject important truths such as the pope's authority.

Five hundred years later, a German monk named Martin Luther had some ideas about what true Christianity was. Some of his views were contrary to what Catholics believe Christ intended for His Church. He and his followers broke with the Catholic Church and formed what is now called Lutheranism. Other men and women had ideas of their own and started their own churches, too. Today there are hundreds (if not thousands) of different Protestant denominations.

There are sincere non-Catholic Christians—Protestant and Orthodox Christians, for instance—who believe many, but not all, of the things we believe as Catholics. Sometimes they may even be more faithful or charitable than many Catholics. That is because the Spirit of Christ is at work in them, too (1 Cor 12:3; CCC 152, 683).

The Catholic view is that the divisions and confusion among Christian communities contradicts the will of Jesus (1 Cor 14:33). He wants His followers to be one (Jn 17:11). We believe the unity Christ desires for His followers only exists fully in the Catholic Church (Eph 4:1–6).

Question #45

"Why does it seem that evangelical Protestant teens have a closer relationship with Jesus than Catholic teens?" Amy M., 16

A. Some evangelical teens do seem to have a closer relationship with Jesus than many Catholic teens. Why? Probably because evangelical churches stress personal conversion more than Catholics typically do. This is unfortunate, because the Catholic Church teaches as strongly as evangelicalism the need for personal conversion (Acts 3:19; Joel 2:12–14; CCC 1430).

Furthermore, evangelicals emphasize an initial conversion experience, when a person steps forward and "accepts Jesus as his or her personal Lord and Savior." This is sometimes known as an "altar call." It can have a profound psychological as well as spiritual effect on a person.

But it is important to remember two things:

First, human experiences and feelings come and go. What matters is one's continuing commitment to follow Jesus, with or without an "experience" (Dt 13:4; Eccl 12:13; Jn 8:12).

Jesus says our love for Him is measured by whether we keep His commandments (Jn 14:15). If we believe, trust, and love Christ by obeying Him, we need not worry about experiences (Jn 14:21–24). A person who claims to have "a personal relationship with Jesus Christ" based on a conversion experience, but who does not keep His commandments *does not* have a close relationship with Christ (1 Jn 1:6; Jas 2:14–26; CCC

162). This is not to say that all or even most evangelicals do not have an authentic relationship with Jesus. It is to say that enthusiasm is not the best way of measuring the quality of our relationship with Christ. The key is always obedience to God's commandments.

Second, Catholics have an "altar call" every week—the call to receive Jesus in the Holy Eucharist. There is no more "personal relationship" we can have with Christ in this life than to be united with Him in the Holy Eucharist (Jn 6:56; CCC 787, 1391, 1406). This relationship should result in personal conversion and serious discipleship.

Question #46

"Why are Protestant kids into the Bible more than Catholics kids?" Amy M., 16

A. Assuming this is true, it is too bad—not for them but for Catholic kids. It means only that Catholic kids aren't being Catholic *enough*. The Catholic Church gave us the Bible and exhorts us to read and study it.

We can see why Protestants would naturally stress the Bible and why Catholics might be tempted to neglect it. The highest authority on earth for the Protestant is the Bible. For the Catholic, the highest authority is the Word of God as it comes to us in the Bible and Sacred Tradition (2 Thess 2:15; 2 Tm 3:16–17; 1 Cor 11:2). Plus, God has given us a divinely guided teacher—the Magisterium of the Church—to help us understand Scripture and Tradition (1 Tm 3:15; Acts 8:30–31; CCC 85, 97, 100). This means we can learn the truths of the Bible without necessarily reading it. The temptation then may be for us to neglect it, which is tragic because

God gave the Bible to us to read (Rom 15:4; 1 Mc 12:9). To ignore it is to ignore a precious gift. In fact, St. Jerome said "Ignorance of Scripture is ignorance of Christ" (*Commentary on Isaiah*, Prologue). As Christians then, we should study Scripture more because of our desire to know more about Christ (2 Tm 3:14–15).

Because Protestant Christians have only the Bible to concern them, they often know it better than most Catholics. (If you only had to study one subject in school, rather than many, imagine how good you would be in that one subject!) When you know the Bible, you can become enthralled with it (Ps 119). This is why Protestant kids are often more "into the Bible" than Catholics. Fortunately, more Catholics kids are now studying Scripture on a regular basis.

Question #47

"Are we allowed to attend an 'all denominations' Christian retreat?" Adrian A., 15

A. It is not necessarily wrong to attend this type of retreat. However, you should be careful, especially if you are not thoroughly grounded in your Catholic faith. This experience could be confusing or even misleading.

Because retreats are often emotional experiences, you might confuse the "good feelings" you have on retreat with truth. Simply because something "feels good" does not mean it is true (Prv 14:12; 2 Tm 4:3-4). Likewise, just because something does not "feel good" does not make it wrong or false (Rom 8:16-18). Feelings are neither true nor false; they are just feelings.

Also, so-called non-denominational or interdenominational events can sometimes be subtly anti-Catholic. Not that the people necessarily intend them to be—they may not even realize it themselves. They just think that being a Christian means believing their way, and they do not always appreciate the fact that Catholics hold other ideas.

It would be wise to ask the leaders a few questions before signing up for the retreat. For example, what do they think about the Catholic Church? Do they believe Catholics are Christians, too? Will you be encouraged to participate in a non-Catholic communion service (in which, as a Catholic, you should not participate)? May you leave at any time during the retreat? Are there Catholics among the retreat leaders?

The answers to these questions should help you decide whether or not it would be wise to take part in the retreat.

Question #48

"What is the difference between the Catholic faith and Mormonism?" Nicole J., 14

A. The basic difference is that Mormonism (also called the Church of Jesus Christ of Latter-day Saints) is a quasi-Christian religion. That means it uses Christian terms like *trinity* and *god* but with very different meanings than traditional Christianity. Sometimes, Mormonism actually contradicts traditional Christian doctrine.

Although Mormons on the whole emphasize the family, morality, and patriotism, their religion denies fundamental Christian beliefs, most notably the existence of one and only one God (Dt 32:39; Is 44:24; CCC 304). They believe there are many gods, made of flesh and bone as we are. They teach that a "worthy" Mormon man (but *not* a Mormon woman) will become a god and rule over his own planet or planets. Mormonism's founder, Joseph Smith, wrote in the book *Teachings of the Prophet*, "God himself was once as we are now, and is an exalted man, and sits enthroned in the heavens" (pp. 345-347). The Catholic faith believes there is only one God and that He has always existed (Gn 21:33; Sir 42:21).

Other Mormon teachings contrary to the Catholic faith include the pre-existence of souls, the revelation of the Book of Mormon, and the Great Apostasy.

Question #49

"Why don't Jehovah's Witnesses celebrate birthdays?" Anastasia B., 14

A. Jehovah's Witnesses do not celebrate birthdays because they believe the only births celebrated in the Bible are those of wicked men. This is simply not true. The birth of Jesus was celebrated by the angels, for example (Lk 2:8–14; CCC 333). Also, John the Baptist's birth was foretold in Scripture and this, of course, would be a moment of great joy (Lk 1:13–17). But even if it were true, that still would not mean we should not celebrate births.

Jehovah's Witnesses also claim birthday celebrations are pagan in origin and therefore wrong. By that logic, they should not refer to the days of the week or the months of the year by their commonly used names because these are of pagan origin.

Moreover, many of the things we practice today came from paganism, but they have been "Christianized." For example, the Church saw value in the pagan practice of exchanging rings at a wedding, and so adopted and blessed it.

Question #50

"Some of my friends are Buddhists. Explain what Buddhism is and what it teaches." Evangeline B., 17

Buddhism was founded by Siddhartha Gautama, known as the *Buddha* (Enlightened One), in southern Nepal in the sixth and fifth centuries before Christ. It is an offshoot of Hinduism. The Buddha is said to have achieved "enlightenment" through meditation. He then gathered a community of monks to carry on his teachings.

Buddhism is basically agnostic on the question of God's existence. It is also more of a philosophy than a religion, since it claims no real divine revelation. Buddhism teaches that through meditation and the practice of good, religious, and moral behavior, one can reach *nirvana* which is the state of enlightenment. Before reaching nirvana, one is subjected to repeated reincarnations. The new life is either good or bad depending on your actions or *karma* from past lives.

There are four "noble truths" (doctrines) of the Buddhist: 1) existence is a realm of suffering; 2) desire and the belief in one's importance cause this suffering; 3) reaching nirvana ends suffering; and 4) nirvana is attained only by meditation and by following the path of righteousness in action and attitude.

Like the Catholic faith, Buddhism is critical of the shallow attempt to find happiness simply by loving the present world. Unlike the Catholic faith, however, Buddhism's goal is not heaven, but the annihilation of desire. Buddha did not know that union with God was possible, so he proposed a sort of spiritual euthanasia whereby one's desire for happiness is to be systematically overcome. Jesus, in stark contrast, teaches us to desire happiness more, not less, than the world urges us to do. He says we should not be satisfied with money, power, and sex because the joys of heaven are so much greater than these things.

Chapter 7

THE CATHOLIC FAITH
AND SOCIETY

Question #51

"Why does the Church always disagree with politics?" Tim H., 16

A. The Church does not "always disagree with politics," although its teachings contradict some people's political ideas or positions. To understand what this means, we should be clear about what politics is: the art of governing a society. People sometimes disagree about the best way to govern society. When they do, their disagreements are political.

For the most part, the Magisterium (the teaching office of the Church) does not advocate specific political programs. You will not find out from the *Catechism* whether there should be farm subsidies, or what to do about welfare, or how to construct a college loan program. Sometimes, however, a moral issue will have political implications. Then the Church does talk about politics, but only because it is obliged to talk about morality (Mt 28:19–20; CCC 407).

Consider, for example, the issue of abortion. Because preborn children are human beings, they have a right to life (Jer 1:5; CCC 2270). Because government is obliged to protect and promote human rights, it is obliged to protect and promote the preborn child's right to life. When government passes laws or makes legal rulings that deny such a basic human right, it is the duty of the Church to speak out. Not because the Church is concerned with the details of politics or favors one political party or another—it does not—but because basic human rights are at stake (Sir 10:19-24; 2 Tm 4:2).

There is a sense, however, in which the Church ought to be fully involved with politics: The Church is not merely the Magisterium but the individual members, especially the laity. Lay men and women are especially called to serve Christ in the world (Mt 5:14–16). This means they should apply their Christian moral values to examining and assessing the laws and practices of society (CCC 2442). They should try their best to foster laws that uphold God's moral law and do away with those that contradict it. Lay people do this by voting, running for office, communicating with elected officials, peacefully protesting and other means. If elected, they would have an obligation to oppose or inhibit, to the limits of their power, any governmental policy or action in violation of the moral or natural law (Jas 4:17).

Doing these things will not always be popular, but then again Jesus said His followers wouldn't be popular with the world (Mt 10:22; Lk 21:16–17; CCC 161, 1821).

Question #52

"What role should the Church play in the world?"
Nathan T., 15

The Church should teach and sanctify the world,

leading it to the One whom God sent as Redeemer and Savior, Jesus (Mt 28:18–20; Jn 17:18; Rom 10:14–15; Mk 16:15–16; CCC 2, 3, 767, 849, 1276).

The Church's teachings are those given by Jesus to the apostles and their successors, the bishops (Mt 10:40; Lk 10:16; CCC 858). The Church sanctifies us by means of the sacraments, which are channels of grace (CCC 1084, 1127, 1131). The Church also sanctifies the world through its lay members who, nourished with the gift of faith and the sacraments, serve as a shining light to the world and as instruments of justice and peace.

Question #53

"If we are supposed to leave everything and follow God, how come our churches are so exquisite and the people within the Church so wealthy?"
Andy B., 15

The passage of Scripture you refer to concerns the need for everyone who would follow Christ to be detached from possessions (Mt 10:37–39, 19:21–24; CCC 226, 2053). For some of us, according to our vocation, this detachment takes the form of giving up personal ownership of material possessions (Mt 6:19; Lk 12:32–34). People who enter religious life do this by taking a vow of poverty. For others, personal possessions may be kept and enjoyed, as long as they are properly used and do not become our "god" (Lk 16:13–14; Eccl 5:18–19).

For some people, like the rich young man in St. Mark's Gospel (Mk 10:17–25), wealth is really an idol—a false god. To follow Christ, such people must turn away from their idol, which may sometimes require them to sell everything. But not everyone can or should do this (Sir 13:23, 31:8–11). Parents, for example, should not give away everything they own. How would they fulfill their God-given responsibility to feed and clothe their children (1 Tm 5:8)? Nevertheless, they should use their possessions with an attitude of willingness to give up everything should it be asked of them (Mt 6:19; CCC 2113, 2424). In short, they should serve God, not money (Mt 6:24).

Regarding the "exquisite" churches and the "wealthy" people who worship in them, several things must be said:

First, there is nothing wrong with having beautiful, well-designed churches. Jesus Himself worshiped in the Jerusalem Temple, which was certainly exquisite and expensive (1 Kgs 6). While He condemned the moneychangers for turning it into a marketplace (Mt 21:12–13; Mk 11:15–17), He never rejected the Temple on the grounds that it was ornate or costly. Also, when Judas objected that the expensive oil used to anoint Christ should be sold and the money given to the poor, Jesus did not agree (Jn 12:3–8). So, we are allowed to spend money, even large amounts, for things that honor God (Lk 16:1–9).

Second, not everyone who attends a beautiful, expensive church is wealthy. A wonderful thing about the great cathedrals and churches is that they are for everyone, poor as well as rich. All are welcome there, where greatness is measured not by how much money one has but by how much love for God and others one has in his heart (Rv 2:9; 1 Cor 1:4–5; Jas 2:1–5; CCC 952).

Question #54

"I don't understand why the pope and bishops live in luxury when they are the servants of Christ."
Michelle P., 15

A. Actually, most bishops do not live in the luxury you suppose. The material resources at their disposal are not for their private benefit but to carry on the mission of the Church. When a bishop retires or resigns, for example, he moves out of the official bishop's residence. He does not own his residence anymore than a former president owns the White House when he leaves office.

You will sometimes hear people accuse our leaders of greed and excess. These people consider things like ornate cathedrals and the art treasures of the Vatican as excessive. But the pope and the bishops do not personally benefit from these things. A cathedral's beauty and the Church's art treasures are for the whole Church—indeed, for all humanity. They are a means of honoring God (1 Kgs 6, 8:12–13).

In the past, it is true that some bishops (and even popes) exploited their offices for personal gain. When this occurred, they deserved rebuke for this sin. Typically, however, popes and bishops seem more conscious of the fact that misuse of wealth not only endangers their own souls but can lead others astray and bring ridicule to the cause of Christ (Sir 31:5–7; Mt 6:24; CCC 2424, 2729).

I personally know of one cardinal who emptied his personal checking account at the end of each year, giving all his money to friends and charities. His aim was to begin each new year with nothing in his personal account. This is a sign of a man who is detached from the material world. I am sure there are many other Church leaders who have a similar detachment from material things.

Question #55

"Why is the Catholic Church negatively portrayed so often in movies and the news?" Dave G., 14

A. There are two perspectives on this question. From an earthly perspective, we can say that the main reason is because the Catholic Church is the moral leader of the world (Mt 28:18–20). It is the voice of reason in an unreasonable age (Mt 5:14–16; Lk 10:16). It stands for truth—and the truth is difficult for many to hear (2 Tm 3:8; Eph 4:17–19; Rom 1:25).

Like Jesus, its founder, the Church calls the world to holiness (Gal 5:13, 16). Most of the world does not want to hear this because the Church challenges it to pursue a higher standard of moral living. It tells people that they cannot steal, lie, cheat, fornicate, kill, and hurt others (Gal 5:19–21). And like Jesus, the Church is persecuted because of its faithfulness to the Gospel (Jn 15:18–25; 1 Jn 3:1; CCC 675).

The second perspective is a heavenly one. The Church is persecuted because it is the body of Christ, and the devil hates it as much as he hates Christ—and for the same reason. St. Paul tells us that we wrestle not with flesh and blood but with powers and principalities, with the devil and his demons (Eph 6:12). In other words, there is a supernatural dimension to the hostility the

Church meets. There are more than merely human wills working actively against us. This would be cause for alarm—if Christ were not for us. But since He is, we can well say, "Who can stand against us?" (Rom 8:31)— not that the world doesn't try its hardest.

In fact, I would probably be nervous if the world stopped persecuting the Church. The Church would then be "too worldly." Remember, Jesus said that whoever follows Him faithfully will be persecuted and even hated (Mt 10:22; Lk 21:17).

Chapter 8

CATHOLIC LIVING

Question #56

"What commitments does one need to make when one becomes a Catholic?" Justin M., 15

A. You need to strive to know, love, and serve God the Father through His Son, Jesus Christ, in the power of the Holy Spirit (Jn 6:27, 17:3; 1 Cor 8:3; CCC 1). You need to commit yourself to being a disciple of Jesus Christ. Since Christ continues to act in the world through the Church with which He is one body, Catholics believe complete discipleship involves adhering to Christ's Word as presented in the teachings of the Catholic Church (Eph 4:11–16).

You need to follow the teachings of the Church. This means assenting to all that the Magisterium (the pope and the bishops united with him) teaches as true concerning faith and morals and, by God's grace, living accordingly (Mt 18:15–18; 2 Thess 3:6; CCC 150, 892). To his disciples Christ said, "Whoever listens to you, listens to Me. Whoever rejects you, rejects Me. And whoever rejects Me, rejects the One who sent Me" (Lk 10:16). The Magisterium carries on this mission. When the Magisterium teaches, it is Christ teaching us through it.

You need to receive Christ's grace through the sacraments. This includes receiving the sacraments of initiation—baptism (Acts 22:16), confirmation (Acts 8:14–19), and the Holy Eucharist (Acts 2:42); the sacraments of healing—reconciliation (Jn 20:21–23) and anointing of the sick (Jas 5:14–15); and those related to the particular vocation to which God is calling you—holy matrimony (Eph 5:31–32) or holy orders (1 Tm 4:14). The sacraments are visible, effective signs of Christ's invisible action (CCC 1113, 1127, 1129).

Finally, Christ exercises His pastoral and kingly authority over His followers through the pastors of His Church (Eph 1:22–23, 4:11–12). You need to obey their lawful authority as a way of obeying Christ (1 Jn 4:6). Following the pastors includes observing the six precepts of the Church (Jn 14:16):

1. Attend Mass on Sundays and Holy Days
   (Ex 31:13–17; CCC 2180).
2. Confess one's sins at least once a year, if one is conscious of mortal sin (Jas 5:14–16; CCC 1457).
3. Receive Holy Communion during the Easter season (Acts 2:42; CCC 1389).
4. Observe appointed days of fasting and abstinence (Acts 13:2–3; CCC 2043).
5. Contribute to the support of the Church
   (Gal 6:6).
6. Observe the marriage laws of the Church
   (Rom 7:2–3).

These precepts are all ways our basic Christian commitment to follow Christ is lived out in His Church.

It is important to remember that these precepts are *minimal* acts of discipleship. Some people adopt a sort of legalistic approach to such requirements and ask "What is the bare minimum I have do?" This is something like a husband asking, "How often do I have to kiss my wife?" This is not a sign of a particularly healthy relationship. The precepts of the Church are more like a sketch, a basic outline of a portrait of a disciple. It is the task of each of us to use the gifts God gives us to fill in that portrait with the oil paint of faith hope, and charity and make it as beautiful as we can.

Question #57

"Can a person truly be a Catholic if he or she is baptized but does not live a Catholic lifestyle?"
Mary B., 13

A. It depends on what you mean by not living a "Catholic lifestyle." Part of a Catholic lifestyle is to believe what the Church teaches (1 Jn 4:6; CCC 892). This is an essential element of being a Catholic. Without faith, it is impossible to be a Catholic, regardless of how "good" a life a person otherwise leads (Heb 11:6).

On the other hand, we may have faith but not put it into practice. In other words, we may lack charity, the love of God and neighbor (1 Cor 13:2). As long as our faith is genuine and our failure to live it "only" a matter of committing sins, we remain Catholics, albeit poor ones (1 Cor 13:2-13).

We should not count too much on the mere fact that we are Catholics, without regard for whether we are in a state of grace and fellowship with God (1 Cor 10:12). One can be a "Catholic" in that sense and still end up separated from God for eternity (Mt 7:21–23; CCC 1821, 2611).

Question #58

"Why is it so important to go to church?"
Ryan H., 15

A. Why is it important for a lover to be with his beloved? If we love God, we will want to spend time with Him in the way He wants us to. God wants us to give ourselves to Him in worship (Col 3:16; Eph 5:18–19; CCC 2096). And He wants us to do it through His Son's own self-surrender and sacrifice, the Eucharist (Lk 22:17–19; CCC 1389). All that requires our going to Church as God commands (Heb 10:25).

Another reason for going to church: We receive special graces by worshiping God and by receiving the Eucharist (Jn 6:56). Going to church can change us and convert our hearts. It can teach us we are not the center of the universe—God is—and He deserves our praise and thanksgiving (Rv 5:12; Ps 145:1–3; CCC 300).

One more point: If we are not worshiping God, we are worshiping something else—ourselves, television, a movie star, or a sports team. Not going to church does not mean we won't worship anything, only that we will worship the wrong thing (CCC 2113).

Question #59

"Is it wrong to practice something like guitar or surfing more than you practice your religion?"
Jared K., 15

A. By "practicing your religion" I assume you mean the actual number of minutes or hours spent in prayer, in study, or at church. No, you are not necessarily required to pray more minutes each day than you surf. We are physical creatures who need relaxation, laughter, friendship, and physical activity.

The real mistake is to assume that time spent doing things you love is somehow the opposite of time spent with God. In fact, surfing and guitar playing can actually glorify God if they are done in an excellent manner because you are being a good steward of the talents and gifts He has given you (Phil 4:8; CCC 1803). We can even practice our faith by doing these types of things if the motive for doing them and the way we do them are correct. They can be offered to God for His glory (Col 3:23).

There is no quota of minutes one has to pray or play each day. Simply keep the following six principles in mind:

1. Strive to do God's will—and want to do His will—more than your own (Lk 22:42; Mt 6:10; CCC 2632).
2. Keep all activities, including your eventual career, in balance with other aspects of life. These activities should not interfere with family relationships or with your basic religious commitments (1 Tm 6:11–12).
3. Make your faith an integral part of your life in all activities. People should know you are a person of integrity no matter what activity you are doing (Mt 5:14–16).
4. Challenge yourself to grow in prayer and in your understanding of God.
5. Set some goals that balance your growth in faith with your growth in life's other activities. (For example, read one religious book for every secular

book you read.) Also, you could pray an extra ten minutes every day that you go surfing.

6. Stay in a state of grace (Jude 21) by avoiding serious sins.

If you keep this type of concern for spiritual growth in mind, you will be on an excellent course towards holiness.

Question #60

"How can I be less hypocritical? I know what Jesus says and what I believe but I often go against these beliefs." Michelle P., 15

A. So does almost everyone in the world. Sts. Peter and Paul and every saint in history (with the exception of Mary), struggled with this very problem (Rom 7:15–25). Here are some practical tips that will help you in this struggle:

• Knowledge is power. If you know your faith, you will know more about how to fight the devil and the temptation to sin (1 Pt 5:8–9; CCC 409).

• Read the lives of the saints. These men and women have been where you are now, and their heroic example will inspire you (Phil 4:9).

• Live a sacramental life. Go to Mass more than just on Sunday, pray the rosary, and go to confession frequently, especially if you have sinned seriously (Heb 10:25; 1 Thess 5:17; CCC 1127, 1129).

• In prayer, ask Jesus for guidance (Mt 7:7).

Question #61

"Why should the pope make our morals and define what is right and wrong?" Rich T., 17

A. The pope does not "make our morals and define what is right and wrong." God does. The pope simply passes on what Jesus taught in the Scriptures and Sacred Tradition (Lk 10:16; Mt 28:18–20; CCC 869).

When a pope is elected, you can bet he is concerned about the awesome task he has been given. He knows the weight of the world rests on his shoulders every day. This great responsibility undoubtedly leads him to prayer many times a day (CCC 936).

Defining and passing on faith and morals to a world tainted with original sin is no fun or easy task. Like rebellious children, many Catholics and non-Catholics alike often do not want to follow what Christ taught (Jn 15:18–25; 1 Jn. 3:1; CCC 844). This makes the pope's job the toughest one in the world. We should pray for the pope everyday that he will continue to persevere in his difficult role as the spiritual shepherd for mankind (1 Thess 5:25; CCC 2636). We should thank God we have a pope to give us a clear understanding of what is and is not true in matters of faith and morals.

Question #62

"What exactly does the commandment 'Honor your father and mother' encompass?" Susan K., 17

A. First, it means obeying your parents because they exercise God-given authority over you (Col 3:20; Eph 6:1–3; CCC 2197). It also means being grateful to your parents for the gift of life (Sir 7:28; Prv 23:22; CCC 2215). And you are to care for your parents when they can no longer care for themselves (Sir 3:12–16; CCC 2218).

Children should obey their parents as long as parental wishes are not contrary to the Catholic faith, while they live in their parents' home, and until they reach adulthood (CCC 2217). After that time, children are still required to love and honor their parents but not necessarily obey them, as they are then old enough to make their own decisions.

The fourth commandment applies to more than just the parent-child relationship. It requires us to obey lawful superiors, including teachers and those who govern (1 Thess 5:12–13). Again, this assumes one is not directed to do something that is contrary to the faith.

The fourth commandment also places a reciprocal duty on parents and those who exercise other forms of authority. Parents should educate and raise their children in the faith (Eph 6:4; CCC 2252). They should respect their children as persons, disciplining them when necessary and providing for their physical, spiritual, educational, and social needs as best they can (1 Tm 5:8). In short, parents are obliged to love their children.

Question #63

"What kind of sin is cussing?" Danny N., 14

A. Cursing, also known as cussing or swearing, is a sin against the second commandment, "Thou shall not take the name of the Lord thy God in vain" (Ex 20:7; CCC 2162). This means that we should never use the names of God or Jesus to express surprise (like, "Oh my God!") or anger.

Nor should we use words to degrade people, who are made in God's image. This is a sin against the fifth commandment, which obliges us to respect other people as persons made in God's image (Ex 20:13; CCC 2164).

Curse words are like little knives that pierce the heart of the Lord. When said with full understanding of their sinfulness, with sufficient reflection, and with full consent of our wills, they are mortal sins (Jas 1:26, 2:7; Lk 6:45). But cursing is usually only venially sinful, because most people do not understand the gravity of their words or because they say them without sufficient reflection (that is, they say them without thinking or as a bad habit).

This is why cursing can be considered a serious sin. To use a name without the proper reverence is to offend the person whose name we are using. In this modern age, we do not understand the glory and majesty of God's name. Several thousand years ago, the Jewish people so honored God's name, *Yahweh*, they *would not even say it*. They came up with a different name for Him—*Adonai* (meaning "Lord"). It would have been considered blasphemy even to say God's name reverently, *let alone as a curse word*. In fact, the only person in Judaism who could lawfully say the name *Yahweh* was the Jewish high priest, and he could say it only *once a year* in the Temple on the Day of Atonement.

We may be desensitized by the harsh things that the modern world presents to us, and we might think it absurd to reverence the name of God. It is not. We are commanded to reverence His name (Lk 1:49; Lv 22:32;

CCC 2144). If we do, our faith will increase. If we do not, we may grow coarse and cold, and we will not grow in our relationship with Jesus.

Question #64

"Is fighting a sin?" John H., 14

A. It depends. If fighting is done out of aggression, especially for the purpose of seriously injuring another person, then it is a grave sin against the fifth commandment, "You shall not kill" (Ex 20:13; CCC 2258). This commandment refers not merely to killing but to any attempt to unjustly harm another person. (*Note*: Some modern translations of the Bible use the word "murder" instead of "kill" in this commandment. "Murder" is actually a more literal translation of the original Hebrew.)

Jesus taught that we should not try to "get even" for attacks on ourselves, even physical attacks, when they involve only ourselves and cause no serious harm. This is really what He meant by "turn the other cheek" (Mt 5:39; Lk 6:29). Jesus' command to "turn the other cheek" means we should not start fights, and we should forgive people's offenses against us. It does not mean, though, that we have to be beaten up by a cruel aggressor.

If attacks on others are also involved or there is a chance of injury to oneself, then the commandment "You shall not kill" does not apply (CCC 2264–65). We can defend ourselves and are obliged to protect others as best we can. We are to use only as much force as necessary to stop an aggressor, however.

Question #65

"Is it a sin to kill animals?" Brant W., 15

A. Animals can justly be used for food, clothing, medical testing, and even, in moderation, for sports (Gn 1:26–30; CCC 307, 2417, 2418). Nevertheless, we should avoid cruelty to animals and any unnecessary infliction of pain upon them (CCC 2418).

Scripture reveals that it was in God's plan for man to subdue and have dominion over the earth (Gn 1:28). However, this position of dominion has to be well-ordered (CCC 339). The *Catechism* says this dominion is "not an arbitrary or destructive domination" (CCC 373). We are not allowed to indiscriminately abuse or kill animals for pleasure. We are stewards, not tyrants, over creation.

While there is nothing wrong with working to prevent cruelty to animals, we should work even harder to defend *human* rights, especially for the most vulnerable among us such as preborn babies, the infirm, and the poor (Mt 25:34–40; CCC 2322).

Question #66

"What can you do to help set your friend straight without losing the friendship?" Kelly A., 15

A. The greatest thing you can do is to tell him or her the truth in love (Jn 8:32). You are not really a friend if you let the person continue living a sinful life (Gal 4:16; 1 Cor 9:16; Acts 20:20). This is "false compassion." We think we are being nice by not saying anything, but we may be helping the person risk losing his or her soul.

The Book of Genesis says we *are* our brother's keeper (Gn 4:9; CCC 900). We *are* responsible for the actions of others to a certain degree. We could be committing a sin of omission if we do not say something. We could be failing to do something we should do as Christians.

I would recommend that you pray, ask other responsible people—such as a priest or parent—for guidance, and then say something to your friend with heartfelt love and compassion (2 Tm 4:1–2; 1 Pt 3:15–16). In the end, that person may appreciate it. Be sure to keep your friend in your prayers after you deliver the message.

Question #67

"How can I convince friends who go to church once or twice a month or just on holidays why they need to go regularly?" Clare H., 14

A. It sounds as if they do not realize what the heart of their professed faith is—a relationship of love with Jesus Christ (Gal 2:20; Eph 3:17–19; CCC 2666). Perhaps you should work on that. You can evangelize your friends by pointing them to Christ (1 Cor 2:2). The best way to do this is not simply by what you say but also by what you do (Mt 5:14–16). Your love for Christ should be evident by how you live. If you are a hypocrite, your friends may see this as proof that going to Mass makes no difference.

As to why they should go to Mass regularly, tell them they should do this as an expression of their love for Christ. This love of Christ means (1) we want to receive Him in the Eucharist (Lk 22:19; CCC 1324) and (2) we will obey Him (1 Jn 3:24). Jesus wants us to gather for corporate worship on Sundays. That is how Christians fulfill the commandment, "Keep holy the Lord's Day" (Heb 10:25).

Jesus says if we love Him, we will keep His commandments (Jn 14:15). Conversely, if we do not keep His commandments, can we really say we love Him (1 Jn 5:18; CCC 2180)?

Remind your friend that God gives us twenty-four hours each day. He gives seven days each week. That's 168 hours a week. We spend about fifty-six hours sleeping and fifty-six hours working or in school. That leaves fifty-six hours for enjoyment and leisure. If we cannot give God one or two hours out of that fifty-six, how serious are we when we say we love Him? And, if we do not love or serve Him in this life, we seriously risk not being with Him in the next (Jn 3:36; CCC 161).

Question #68

"What can we do to promote living a more Catholic lifestyle to nominal Catholics?" Therese J., 15

A. Live the faith yourself with conviction (Mt 5:14–16). Don't be "lukewarm." Also, have the courage to explain the practical reasons for living the Faith. If you don't know these reasons, learn them (1 Pt 3:15; CCC 2032, 2037). Explain how the Church's moral teachings protect us from physical and spiritual harm (1 Thess 5:12–13).

If this does not work, you may have to verbally "hit them between the eyes" with the tough message offered by Scripture. Tell them what Jesus says about those who are lukewarm. In the book of Revelation, Jesus says: "So, because you are lukewarm, neither hot nor cold, I will spit you out of my mouth" (Rv 3:16). Other translations have used the phrase "vomit you out of my mouth." Tell your friends that if they die in a state of apathy towards God, they seriously risk an eternity *without* the One they ignored in life (Mt 7:13–14, 21–23; CCC 1036).

Question #69

"Many of my friends and even strangers try to question my faith. I have tried to debate with them, but you can't argue with people who have their minds made up. What do you suggest I say in reply?" Jessica N., 14

A. Yes, you can argue with people who have their minds made up. You simply have to come up with better arguments (1 Pt 3:15; CCC 2145).

You first need to ask them if they are *really* interested in having a discussion or are they debating simply for the sake of debating. If they are interested in discussing the issues, you then need to thoroughly know their positions. Be a good listener and be charitable. Do not be too defensive.

If you do not have an answer, be frank and tell them so (Prv 12:17). But also tell them that you will get back to them *and then do so*. Stay on one issue at a time. Don't let the person jump from issue to issue. Write down what you have resolved so you will not have to re-address the same issues again.

Pray that the Holy Spirit will guide you and that you will remain humble (Jn 14:26; Prv 11:2; CCC 153, 179).

Be sure to pray that your friends receive the gift of faith. Faith is a gift (Eph 2:8–9). Believing in the Catholic Church is a gift. All the arguments in the world will not convince people without God's grace. So, pray to God that they receive this grace and respond to it.

Question #70

"How can youth leaders get Catholic teens more excited about God in their youth groups or in their church?" Amy M., 16

A. When I was a former youth minister, I worked with many kids who could be classified as "lukewarm." They didn't seem to care too much about religion. They were bored in religious education classes. They were probably apathetic because they were not convinced about the truths of the faith.

I recommend trying to get teens fully convinced about *just one issue*, perhaps abortion. After they come to see that truth exists and that it is vitally important, you can then introduce them to other truths. You can convince them that "objective truth" exists and that we need to act on this truth (Jn 8:32; CCC 2466). They will start to see the ridiculousness of the "live and let live" mentality (CCC 89). How can one let an Adolf Hitler "do his own thing?" How can one sit by as millions of babies are killed each year in abortion?

An energetic, even mildly confrontational faith will excite teens. Then you can introduce them to a deeper sacramental and contemplative approach to the Faith (1 Cor 3:1–2; CCC 1133, 2030).

Question #71

"Is it OK for Catholics to listen to non-Christian music?" Amy M., 16

A. Sure, as long as it is done in moderation and the music does not contain lyrics that are sexually explicit, violent, or cruel. Although people say, "I don't listen to the lyrics; I just like the music," the message still gets through. There is no way we can constantly expose ourselves to explicit media and not be influenced by it. Listening to music that contains lyrics contrary to the Christian faith may desensitize you to worldly thinking and lead you into sin. Therefore, you should be cautious (2 Pt 1:5–8).

A good rule of thumb when deciding on whether certain music is not spiritually dangerous is to ask, "Would Jesus listen to this music for relaxation" (2 Thess 3:7, 9; Rom 13:14; CCC 1803)? If the answer is "no," then you should stay away from it (Phil 4:8; CCC 2830).

Question #72

"How does one become a saint?" Thang P., 19

A. One becomes a saint by doing the will of God, which is another way of saying loving God above everything else (Mt 10:32–33, 22:37–40). This includes living a sacramental life, practicing the virtues, especially humility (Gal 6:3; Mk 10:15; CCC 1389, 2180), and daily prayer (1 Thess 5:17).

A sacramental life should include frequent Mass (at least on Sunday, if not a few times each week) and frequent confession (perhaps once a month and immediately after serious sin).

A virtuous life includes striving for perfection in faith, hope and charity (1 Cor 13:13; Rom 15:13). Faith is believing in things not fully seen (Heb 11:1); hope is trusting in the promises of our Lord Jesus (Heb 3:5–6); and charity is the act of loving God and others (1 Jn 4:7–8). Continual striving for perfection in these areas, along with living a sacramental life, will put you on course for sainthood (1 Thess 5:14–22; CCC 1084).

You may also consider meeting regularly with a spiritual director. Meeting with an older brother or sister in the faith such as a priest or religious sister will help you learn from another's experiences and wisdom (1 Thess 5:12–13; CCC 1269). Meeting with one person on a regular basis will allow him or her to get to know you, your personality, strengths, and struggles. Your spiritual director will then be able to offer better and more specific recommendations on how you can strengthen your walk with Jesus.

Chapter 9

CATHOLIC BELIEFS
AND PRACTICES

Question #73

"Does baptism make a baby a friend of God?"
Ravi D., 17

A. In baptism a baby is made a *child* of God. Like circumcision in the Old Testament, baptism makes the baby a member of the family of God (Col 2:11–14; Jn 3:3–5; CCC 804). However, baptism is more powerful than circumcision because it is built on a better foundation—Jesus Christ and the new covenant He established (Heb 8:6–7).

In fact, baptism does at least three things for the one being baptized:

1. It unites him or her to Jesus Christ (Gal 3:26–27; CCC 790).

2. By infusing sanctifying grace, baptism gives supernatural life to a soul previously dead because of original sin. (Sanctifying grace is necessary for salvation.) In adults, baptism also removes actual sins that were committed before baptism (Rom 6:3–5, 11; Col 2:11–14; CCC 405, 1263–66).

3. It makes the baptized person a member of the Church (Jn 3:3–5; CCC 1267).

Question #74

"I thought we receive the Holy Spirit in confirmation, yet I heard we also receive Him in baptism. How can we receive what we already have? Do we just receive a blessing in baptism?" Nicholas, 14

A. We receive the Holy Spirit first in baptism and then again in a fuller way at confirmation. At baptism, the Holy Spirit is sent to wash away original sin and bring the soul into a state of grace (Acts 2:38 22:16; CCC 1226, 1262). You receive the life of the Blessed Trinity, dwelling within you and making you a child of God.

Prior to baptism, due to the effects of original sin, the soul is lacking the sanctifying grace necessary for eternal life (Rom 5:12–14; CCC 1267). At baptism, we are joined with Christ, and therefore we become members of his Body, the Church (Ti 3:5–7).

In confirmation we receive different graces which prepare us to be adult Christians. In this sacrament, we are given the grace of the Holy Spirit to embark on our apostolic mission to the world. We receive a special grace that enables us to more boldly live and profess our faith (Acts 8:14–19, 19:1–6; CCC 1285). We are enrolled as soldiers in the Church's spiritual army. Confirmation also strengthens the graces and gifts we received at baptism (2 Cor 1:21–22; CCC 1303). The grace in confirmation is more "tailor made" for this next stage of our life of faith.

Question #75

"If a baby is aborted and was never baptized, will it go to heaven?" Ravi D., 17

A. We do not know for sure. The *Catechism of the Catholic Church* says the following: "As regards children who have died without Baptism, the Church can only entrust them to the mercy of God, as she does in her funeral rites for them. Indeed, the great mercy of God, Who desires that all men should be saved, and Jesus' tenderness toward children which caused Him to say: 'Let the children come to Me, do not hinder them' (Mk 10:14), allow us to hope that there is a way of salvation for children who have died without Baptism" (CCC 1261). It is worth noting that the unbaptized babies of Bethlehem are honored as saints in the Church on the Feast of the Holy Innocents (December 28) and are certainly in heaven as martyrs for Jesus. A Catholic can hope that God likewise welcomes as martyrs the little ones who have been murdered by the crime of abortion, an act that is radically opposed to the gospel of life.

Question #76

"Why do we have to go to confession? Why can't we just go to God for forgiveness?" Genny C., 13

A. God has given us the awesome gift of confession because He wants to reach us through the Church, the community of believers (1 Thess 5:12–13). God wants us to be a family (1 Tm 3:15), so He gave us spiritual fathers in the priesthood. The priests have the authority to administer His forgiveness to us (CCC 1461). "Whose sins you forgive, they are forgiven. Whose sins you retain, they are retained," Jesus told the apostles (Jn 20:23). In short, confession is one of Christ's gifts to us. It is a wonderful spiritual treasure, a great gift we should rejoice in.

Actually, we can go "directly" to God, but also through His Church. God sees the two as necessarily linked (Lk 10:16; CCC 858). Our sin, even if we suppose it is only "against God," robs our fellow believers of something—of our being in communion with God and them. Sin diminishes the power of the Church because it cuts us off from full communion together in the Holy Spirit (CCC 953). We become like a dead limb, just barely hanging on, and dead limbs can be harmful to the tree (Rom 11:20–22).

The Church is a body (Eph 5:23 CCC 817). When one member suffers, the whole body suffers. To be reconciled, we must not only repent before God; we must also have reconciliation with the Church. That is the way God wants it (CCC 1469).

Remember what Jesus said we must do if we are making an offering to God and we recall that someone has a grievance against us? He said we should be reconciled with our brother first, then make our offering to God (Mt 5:21–26). Why is that? Because reconciliation with God and reconciliation with His people are tied together.

Confession also helps us grow in the virtue of humility. Humility is the first step towards true repentance (Mt 23:12). Because pride is the root of all sin, an act of humility, such as confessing to a priest, will help push pride out of our lives (Ez 6:49–50). St. Teresa of Avila described humility as "honesty." If we are humble, we are able to honestly focus on our faults.

A priest can keep us more objective about our sins. He can also give us a concrete "plan of action" to avoid sin in the future. If we go directly to God in the privacy of our own home, we can deceive ourselves. We can be either too harsh or too lenient.

Question #77

"If God knows everything we do, then how come we have to go to confession?" Amber H., 19

A. We go to confession to say "I'm sorry" for our sins, not to tell God something He does not already know. You may know your younger brother broke your CD player, but wouldn't it be aggravating if he knew you knew, but still did not say "I'm sorry?" It would be a double slap in the face.

In addition to saying "sorry" to God, confession also reconciles us with the Church (CCC 1469). There is no such thing as a private sin. Every sin affects the world in a negative manner. There is always a ripple effect.

When a Catholic accepts and takes advantage of the sacrament of reconciliation, he builds up the body of Christ (Col 1:24; CCC 1496). He is implicitly saying, "I believe in the sacrament, and you should, too." This affirmation of the sacrament can lead others to live a sacramental life (2 Cor 8:21).

Question #78

"Doesn't God forgive you no matter what? Therefore, isn't confession unnecessary?" Emily F., 15

A. What you are asking is, "Doesn't God just 'look the other way' when we sin?" Or, if He really loves us, why does He let our sins get in the way of our relationship with Him? Why does He demand repentance first? Why can't He forgive us unconditionally?

The answer is that forgiveness, by its very nature, requires acceptance on the part of the one forgiven in order to be complete. The goal of forgiveness is reconciliation (CCC 1455). The person who admits no fault can accept no forgiveness for it and therefore cannot be reconciled with the one he has offended by his action (Lk 13:3; 2 Cor 7:10).

Because God is holy, He cannot just "ignore" our sin (Ps 113:4). Sin hurts us, and God does not want us to be hurt unnecessarily (Tb 12:10). He loves us too much to leave us in our sin (Jer 4:22; CCC 1423). The only way out is repentance.

Furthermore, sin itself keeps us from God, who is our ultimate happiness, as long as we are unrepentant (Is 59:1–2, Lam 3:42–44; CCC 387). If we think of sin as merely breaking the rules, especially rules seen as arbitrarily laid down by God, then it is hard to understand why God cannot just "look the other way." But if sin is understood as preferring some lesser good (*something* else or *someone* else, including ourselves) to God, the supreme Good, then

God's love for us demands that He set us straight. He requires us to turn back to Him—for our sake, not His. God wants us to turn our hearts from the lesser good to Himself, our supreme Good (Heb 12:5–11; CCC 1458).

The sacrament of reconciliation is the normal means God has established for us to come back to Him if we sin seriously after baptism (Jas 5:16; CCC 1422). Confession is an expression of God's love for us, for He knows our hearts and our need to confess.

Question #79

"Doesn't confession give people the idea that it is all right to sin as long as you are sorry later?"
Emily F., 15

A. There is no reason it should. People who think that way are mistaken, due either to ignorance or choice.

Confession means God's forgiveness is available if we repent, not that it is OK to sin so long as you repent (Rom 6). Would you intentionally break your arm because you knew a doctor could fix it later?

We should never sin thinking we need not worry because God will forgive us later. That itself is the sin of presumption, presuming God's mercy regardless of His commandments (Rom 6:23; CCC 1006).

Sin involves turning our backs on God in some way (Jer 5:25; CCC 472). We should never try to "use" God by turning away from Him *now* assuming that *later* we will turn back to Him (Rom 11:19–22). Why?

First, because sinning this way casts doubt about the sincerity of our later repentance. True repentance involves genuine sorrow for having sinned and the willingness never to do it again. How likely is it that we will truly be repentant—sorry for having sinned to begin with—if all along we thought to ourselves that we would enjoy sin now and repent later?

Second, how do we know that "later" will ever come? Death could come at any time. What if it comes before we are sorry or repentant?

It is very dangerous to live a life of serious and frequent sin. Though superficial, sin is very attractive and can be addictive (Rom 7:22–23; CCC 2542). A person can get caught up in a certain way of living without even knowing the magnitude of the problem. One can get hooked on a particular sin and not know how enslaved he or she really is to that sin (Rom 6:16).

We should be constantly on guard against sin. And we should try to avoid even those things that may "lead us into temptation," as we pray in the Lord's prayer. The Church calls these "occasions of sin," things that are not sinful in themselves but which may lead us into sin.

For example, if a person has a drinking problem, a bar would be an "occasion of sin" because it is a place where alcohol is served freely and openly. The bar itself is not evil, but it is a place of temptation. It is just not a smart place for a person with a drinking problem to be.

Question #80

"Is a priest necessary for forgiveness in confession, or will God forgive you as soon as you are sorry for the sin?" Ravi D., 17

A. When we sin seriously, we lose sanctifying grace and cut ourselves off from God (Is 59:1–2). When this happens, God gives "actual grace" to work on our conscience to bring us back to Him (Jn 6:44; CCC 2000). If we realize our sin at this point and repent, and by repentance I mean that we have perfect contrition (CCC 1452) for our sins, which means supernaturally loving God above all things for His sake—then we are on our way back home. If we should die at that point, our sins would be forgiven. But otherwise we are still obliged to confess our sins to a priest (Jas 5:16; CCC 1493).

Why? Because God has willed that we use the sacrament of confession, even if we have already made an act of perfect contrition. In fact, an act of perfect contrition, for a Catholic, involves the firm resolution to get to confession as soon as possible.

Sin requires reconciliation with the Church as well as with God, as we have seen (Jn 20:21–23; CCC 1469). An act of perfect contrition may reconcile us to God, but He still expects us to seek reconciliation with the Church.

Furthermore, if we are truly reconciled to God through perfect contrition, we will implicitly want to do His will, which includes going to confession as soon as we can (Jn 14:15). If we say that we are perfectly contrite for a serious sin but do not bother with confession, we are kidding ourselves.

Question #81

"Does God forgive us even when we do not forgive ourselves?" Erinn T., 16

A. Yes, assuming we have gone to confession or have made an act of perfect contrition in an emergency situation (CCC 1452).

There are a few reasons why people do not "forgive themselves" after confession. Some people suffer from *scrupulosity*, which is a disease of the soul in which the person never "feels" forgiven. This can often be remedied by spiritual counseling. Others simply need more catechetical instruction on the power of the sacrament and how God completely blots out our sin when we seek forgiveness (Is 43:25, 44:22; Acts 3:19; CCC 674).

It is important to remember that the sacraments transmit God's saving grace whether we "feel" it or not. As long as we are truly sorry for and repent of our sins, God will forgive us (Ez 33:14–16).

Question #82

"Can you be forgiven for committing murder?" Tom S., 14

A. Yes, if you are truly sorry. The only unforgiveable sin is final impenitence, which is a rejection of God and his mercy even up to death. This is referred to in Scripture as the "unforgivable sin" against the Holy Spirit (Lk 12:10; CCC 1864).

Question #83

"Is it a sin to go to communion after having been sexually active with someone if you ask God for forgiveness in your heart (but do not go to confession)? Will you go to hell for this?"
Name and age withheld

A. To begin, I assume you are not married to the person with whom you are sexually active.

It is a sin to go to communion if you have serious sin on your soul and have not asked for forgiveness from God through the ordinary means He established— confession to a priest (Jas 5:16; Jn. 20:23 CCC 1415).

St. Paul says very clearly in his first letter to the Corinthian Catholics that a person who "eats the bread and drinks the cup of the Lord unworthily will have to answer for the body and blood of the Lord" (1 Cor 11:27; CCC 1385). In the culture of the time, the Corinthians would have clearly understood what St. Paul meant: If one receives the Eucharist unworthily, such a person is guilty of killing the Lord.

St. Paul goes on to say that anyone "who eats and drinks without discerning the body (of the Lord), eats and drinks judgment upon himself" (1 Cor 11:29). As you see, St. Paul is very serious about the need to be in a state of grace when you receive the Eucharist.

If you commit a serious sin, sexual or otherwise, you should ask God for forgiveness immediately (Lk 5:8; Dn 9:4–5). But you should also make every reasonable

116 Did Adam & Eve Have Belly Buttons?

effort to go to confession before attending Mass. If you have not received the sacrament of reconciliation, you should refrain from receiving the Eucharist until you have done so.

You should still attend Mass on Sundays and participate in other aspects of the liturgy (Ex 20:8–11; CCC 418), but not receive the Eucharist until you have received the sacrament of reconciliation. You can express repentance by worshiping God at Mass, taking part in the penitential rite, and listening to His Word proclaimed in the readings (CCC 1190).

Furthermore, you should seek "spiritual communion" with Jesus at Mass. This is a form of communion with Him through prayer alone, when one cannot approach and receive Jesus in the Eucharist. You should say a prayer like this: "Jesus, I cannot receive You today, but I wish You to dwell in me."

As for whether you will go to hell, that depends on whether you are in state of grace when you die (Mt 7:21–23). The Bible makes it clear that receiving communion unworthily is not a small matter. It is a serious sin, a sacrilege. Also, we should not presume we can sin habitually and still get to heaven.

Question #84

"How do you determine if you can receive communion or not?" Angela R., 15

A. By examining your conscience to determine, as best you can, whether you are in a state of grace. If you have committed any mortal sins that have not been confessed, you are not in a state of grace (1 Cor 11:28).

If you are in a state of grace, you can and should receive the Eucharist. If you are not, you should not receive it. To do so would be the sin of sacrilege (1 Cor 11:27; CCC 1385).

As you grow in the spiritual life, you will generally find it easier to determine whether you have committed any mortal sins (1 Jn 3:19–24, 4:13). In the meantime, here is a quick lesson on what constitutes a mortal sin.

A mortal sin is a grievous offense against God that deprives the sinner of sanctifying grace, which is the supernatural life of the soul (1 Jn 5:16–17; CCC 1855). It also makes the person an enemy of God, takes away the merits of one's good actions done in a state of serious sin, and deprives one of the sanctifying grace necessary for salvation (Rom 1:18; Prv 15:9; CCC 1861).

To commit a mortal (or deadly) sin, there are three conditions that must be present:

1. The thought, word, action, or omission must be seriously wrong or considered seriously wrong.
2. The sinner needs to know it is seriously wrong.
3. The sinner must give full consent of the will in choosing the sin (CCC 1857, 1874).

I have included an examination of conscience at the end of this book. Cut it out or photocopy it and keep it with you. This will help you determine whether you have committed a serious offense against God. As you become more sensitive to God's laws (through prayer, study and frequent reception of the sacraments), you will know almost immediately when you have committed a serious offense.

Question #85

"At Mass, how is the bread and wine God's Body and Blood? When I see the bread, I don't see flesh or skin. Also, the wine is not thick enough to be blood." John D., 14

A. You are right that in the Eucharist we do not see the flesh and blood of Christ in their natural forms. That's because the Eucharist is a *sacrament*, which means it is a *sign* (1 Cor 11:26; CCC 1130-31). The sign can be discerned (seen, heard, felt, tasted, or touched) but not Christ's actual flesh. So we have to have faith in the invisible reality (Jn 20:29).

For example, you cannot see your sins being forgiven in baptism. All you see is water being poured on you (and all you feel is wet). Yet we really and truly have our sins removed with baptism (Acts 2:38, 22:16; CCC 265). We can discern (feel) the water. We have to have faith that the forgiveness of sins actually took place.

In the case of the Eucharist, all we see are the appearances of bread and wine. The invisible reality is Christ's glorified Body and Blood, His soul and divinity (Lk 22:19–20; Mt 26:26–28; CCC 1413).

Things we encounter have *substance* and *accidents*. *Substance* refers to the thing itself that exists *in itself* rather than as an *aspect* of something else. A tree, a car, and a human being are "substances" in this sense. But these things also have certain qualities or characteristics that do not exist on their own but *in* them.

Think of it this way: A tree may have green leaves or brown. A car may be red or green. A human may be tall or short. These characteristics are real, but they don't exist on their own; they exist as attributes of *other* things. We never, for instance, run into "redness" or "tallness." These qualities exist, but only in things that are red or tall—that car or that boy. We call such qualities the *accidents* (in technical language, not in the ordinary sense of the word, that is, something unintended).

The Eucharist has both substance and accidents. When the priest consecrates the Eucharist, the accidents of bread and wine remain while their substance is changed into the Body and Blood of Christ. The Eucharist looks like bread and wine and tastes like bread and wine, but has really and truly changed into the Body and Blood of Christ (1 Cor 10:16, 11:23–25; CCC 1375).

Ordinarily a change of substance would mean a change in accidents, for the accidents of a thing usually go along with the substance. But in the Eucharist God supernaturally maintains the accidents of bread and wine (the color, shape, taste, smell, etc.) despite changing their substance to that of the Body and Blood of Christ (CCC 1374).

Why does God retain the accidents of bread and wine? For at least five reasons:

1. God reminds us that Christ is the source of our spiritual as well as physical life by using the appearance of bread and wine, which help give us physical life (Jn 6:55–58). God often links the physical and spiritual together.

2. God becomes one with us physically as we eat the Eucharistic elements. This communion is a means of

joining with us spiritually (Jn 6:56; 1 Cor 10:16; CCC 1416). Jesus literally takes on the accidents normal to bread and wine, while keeping his divine/human substance. He does this with the accidents of bread and wine, which are taken into our bodies to become part of us.

3. The elements of bread and wine are taken from the Passover meal of the Hebrews (Lk 22:15; CCC 1409).

Thus God links the Eucharist to His covenant with the Jewish people. The elements of bread and wine are taken from the Passover meal of the Hebrews (Lk 22:15; CCC 1409).

4. God wants to link the Eucharist with every meal. When food is blessed, we acknowledge God as Lord of our lives and of creation. The Eucharist is the supreme act of acknowledgment (1 Cor 11:26), for in it we offer God's supreme gift to us, Jesus, back to Him. And with the Eucharist, we also offer ourselves to God.

5. As St. Augustine says, the Eucharist, in keeping the appearance of bread and wine, reminds us that "from many grains we are made one loaf; from many grapes, one vintage" (*Sermo* 227.1).

Question #86

"Do any other Christian faiths have communion?"
Elisabeth G., 18

A. Most Christian churches have some form of communion. But with a few rare exceptions, only the Eastern Orthodox have the same Eucharist as the

Roman Catholic Church—the Body and Blood of Christ made present under the appearances of bread and wine. Like Catholic priests, Orthodox priests have valid priestly orders (because they have validly consecrated bishops), so they are able to celebrate a valid liturgy in which God changes bread and wine into the Body and Blood of Christ.

The Protestant faiths have a variety of views on this question. Lutherans, for example, believe in a form of the real presence—that Jesus' body and blood are present *along with* the "substance" of bread and wine—a view the Catholic Church rejects (CCC 1376). Most evangelical and fundamentalist Protestants deny any form of the real presence of Jesus in communion. They teach that Jesus is either only "spiritually" present, as He is at other times when Christians gather, or symbolically present, with the bread and wine simply *representing* Him. The Catholic Church rejects these views as incomplete at best (Jn 6:55; 1 Cor 11:29; CCC 1373, 1375).

Question #87

"Is Christ more present in the Eucharist than He is in society?" Ravi D., 17

A. First we need to be clear about how Jesus is present in society.

Jesus is present in society because He is God, and God is everywhere and in everything by His power, essence, and knowledge (Jer 23:23–24).

Jesus is also present in society because each person is made in God's image and Jesus is the supreme embodiment of that image (Gn 1:27; Col 1:15; CCC 1701).

That is why He could say of the poor, "Whatever you do to the least of these ... you do to me" (Mt 25:40).

And Jesus is present in society through His Holy Spirit calling all to communion with the Father in the Church (Jn 15:26–27).

Finally, Christ is present in society insofar as He is in the Church herself: in His Word, in His people, in His priests, and above all, in the Holy Eucharist (Mt 18:19–20; CCC 1373).

In the Eucharist, however, Christ is present in a much more profound way than He is in society as a whole. In society He is present in a purely spiritual manner. Though the Eucharistic Presence of Christ is, in a sense, concealed by the appearances of bread and wine, Jesus Christ is really, truly, and substantially present there, Body, Blood, Soul, and Divinity (Jn 6:55; CCC 1374).

This is why we genuflect before the tabernacle at church: Christ is present there in a unique way. This is why we show reverence when approaching Holy Communion (CCC 1418). This is why we have Eucharistic adoration, worshiping the Eucharistic Christ as God. And this is why we kneel at the consecration, bending our knees before the God who made us.

How great a mystery it is that in the Eucharist, the Creator, Savior, and Lord of the universe comes to us, His mere creatures, in the form of food for our bodies. And He is truly food for our souls as well (Jn 6:56).

Question #88

"What is confirmation?" Tara O., 14

A. Confirmation is one of the three sacraments of initiation; the others are baptism and the Holy Eucharist (CCC 1212). These sacraments make us part of—or more fully part of—Christ's Church.

Confirmation is the sacrament by which the Holy Spirit comes to us in a radical way after baptism to strengthen us (*confirmation* means "strengthening"), to increase and deepen the grace of our baptism and to make us "soldiers for Christ." Through the sacrament of confirmation, we are specially equipped to spread and defend the faith by word and deed, as witnesses of Jesus (Acts 8:14–19, 19:1–6; CCC 1285, 1316).

The bishop usually confers the sacrament, though priests can also do so in special circumstances with permission (CCC 1313, 1314). The minister of the sacrament extends his hands over those to be confirmed, prays over them and anoints them with holy oil (CCC 1320).

Oil is used because it is a symbol of strength. In ancient times, athletes used oil to limber up their muscles to prepare for the contest. In spiritual terms, we are being prepared for the spiritual contest ahead of us.

All too often young people are apathetic to confirmation. Perhaps this is because of poor catechetical instruction or because they are overstimulated with television, movies, and popular culture. Either way, they need to know that the things of God are not to be taken lightly. I suspect that when we get to heaven, we will see the crucial role our confirmation played in bringing us to eternal peace and happiness with God.

Question #89

"Why did God make marriage one of the seven sacraments?" Joel O., 13

A. Christ gave us the sacraments as ordinary means of receiving His grace. He used commonplace things like water (for baptism), oil (for confirmation and anointing of the sick), and bread and wine (for the Holy Eucharist) so the sacraments would be readily available to us. More importantly, He made holy these ordinary, earthly things by using them in special ways. Marriage is one of those ordinary things that Christ elevated to the supernatural level and made a means of grace (Mk 10:2–12; CCC 1084, 1210).

Why marriage is important should be obvious. It provides a place for children to come into being with the irreplaceable love only two parents, committed to each other as well as their children, can give (CCC 1601, 1604). More than this, though, marriage is one of the images God uses to portray his relationship with the Church. That is why Jesus spoke of heaven as a wedding banquet and performed his first miracle at a wedding (Jn 2). That is why Paul tells us that marriage is an image of Christ and the Church (Eph 5:22–31). And that is why the New Testament concludes with the great marriage feast of the Lamb (Rv 19:9).

Question #90

"What is considered a valid Catholic marriage in the eyes of the Catholic Church? Does the ceremony need to be officiated by a priest?"
Susan K., 17

A. There are several components that need to be present in order for a marriage to be valid. They are "capacity," "consent," and "form." If one of these is missing, for either of the two parties, the marriage is not valid. Let me explain each:

"Capacity" is the *ability* to get married. Impediments that would go against capacity include one's age or being already married (CCC 1625).

"Consent" is the act of freely giving oneself to the other. The two people must *mean* the words they are saying in the ceremony. If someone is planning not to allow the children to be raised Catholic or planning to "try out" marriage to see if it works, he or she is not consenting fully, and the marriage would probably be invalid. Psychological immaturity or a gross misunderstanding of the nature of marriage are also conditions that may hinder one's valid consent. Many annulments have been granted in recent years because of a lack of consent by at least one of the two parties (CCC 1628).

"Form" is the issue of *how* the marriage is contracted. A marriage before a justice of the peace is not valid for a Catholic. A marriage without an official representative of the Church (that is, a priest or deacon) and two witnesses would not be valid (CCC 1630–31).

The book *100 Answers to Your Questions on Annulments* (Ascension Press) by Dr. Edward Peters, a canon and civil lawyer, offers clear answers on marriage and annulments. If you want more specifics, this is the book for you. This book is listed in the Resources section.

Question #91

"Does the Church advise against marrying a non-Catholic?" Helen M., 17

A. The Church encourages marriages between Catholics and warns against the added difficulties that can accompany "mixed" marriages (marriages between a Catholic and a baptized non-Catholic) and what are called marriages with "disparity of cult" (marriages between a Catholic and a non-baptized person) (CCC 1633).

There are serious dangers in a mixed marriage. The couple risks bringing the issues of Christian disunity into their marriage and family life. Catholics and non-Catholic Christians often have profound differences on matters of doctrine, morality, sacramental worship, and church practice that can pose grave problems, especially with respect to raising children. Problems are even more severe when Catholics and non-Christians marry (2 Cor 6:14–16; CCC 1634).

Here is another reason to avoid a mixed marriage: When a Catholic marries a non-Catholic, the *Catholic* might have a more difficult time practicing his or her faith. The two people are not taking advantage of the most valuable marital resources available: God and His Church. When questions of morality, finances, the raising of children, or other important issues arise, the spouses may approach the problem from different perspectives. This can even happen to two Protestant Christians who worship in different denominations.

Because the Church has two-thousand years of collective wisdom on this topic, it knows the challenges and sacrifices that couples face. When both parties have a devotion to the Eucharist and to Our Lady and take advantage of frequent confession, they are well equipped to handle problems due to the special grace that comes their way.

Catholics need the express permission of Church authorities to lawfully marry a non-Catholic Christian, and the same to validly marry a non-Christian (CCC 1635). For more information, you should speak to your pastor.

Question #92

"Can a Catholic be married to a Protestant without the Protestant converting first? If so, how?" Mary B., 13

A. Yes. Although it would most likely help the marriage if the Protestant did embrace the faith, it is not mandatory. Some theologians may even say it would be better to marry a fervent Protestant (as long as he or she is not anti-Catholic) than a nominal Catholic. However, your best bet in almost all cases is to find someone with whom you share a deep Catholic faith.

If a Catholic marries a baptized, non-Catholic Christian, the two need to follow the laws of the Church regarding marriage. One of these laws is the commitment to raise the children Catholic (CCC 1635).

Question #93

"Why can't people get divorces in the Catholic Church?" Andy D., 13

A. Divorce is spiritually impossible, according to Jesus (Mk 10:1-12). It is not merely "against the rules." It is like trying to repeal the law of gravity, not like trying to repeal a parking ticket.

Jesus' command against seeking divorce is not an arbitrary "rule," but rather a comment on what marriage actually *is*. A valid marriage is simply not capable of being dissolved. A validly married couple who divorce may *think* their action has ended their marriage before God and in the eyes of the Church, but that is not true. They are still married (Rom 7:2–3; 1 Cor 7:10–11; CCC 2382).

Divorce and remarriage violate natural and divine laws. They break the covenant to which the spouses freely consented—namely to live with each other until the death of one of them (Mk 10:2–12; Gn 2:23–24; CCC 1665, 2384). Divorce also introduces disorder into the family and into society as a whole. This can bring great harm to one or both of the spouses and certainly to the children (CCC 2385).

Divorce needs to be distinguished from *annulment*. An annulment is an official declaration that what *appeared* to be a marriage was not in fact a true marriage because it lacked some necessary element.

The sacrament of matrimony expresses the relationship between Christ and His Church. Christ is no bigamist— He is "Bridegroom" of only one "bride," the Church.

So, too, in marriage. Spouses are to be exclusively committed to one another, so remarriage after divorce is similar to polygamy (having more than one spouse) (Lk 16:18; CCC 2387).

Question #94

"When and why can one get an annulment?"
Katie V., 14

A. Annulments are granted by a Church court (called a *tribunal*) when it is determined that no valid marriage exists between a couple. This is due to the lack of some necessary element at the time of the marriage on the part of one or both parties: a lack of true consent, the capacity to marry, or proper form (CCC 1629).

Question #95

"Could a woman who is abused by her husband get an annulment?" Gabriela S., 17

A. Only if the "marriage" was not valid to begin with (CCC 1629). Spousal abuse *may* be an indicator of other problems that were present when the marriage was contracted which invalidated it, but this is by no means certain. It is possible that someone in a valid marriage later chose to become abusive.

In an abusive situation where the marriage is valid, an annulment is not possible, although it may be necessary for the abused spouse to separate from the abuser. A spiritual advisor or counselor (such as a priest) may recommend a temporary or even indefinite separation because of the danger to one or both of the involved parties. The hope is that the abuser would repent and the marriage could be saved. However, if the separation ends up being an extended one, neither spouse is free to remarry (Lk 16:18; CCC 2383).

Again, the abuse may be a symptom of some deeper problem. This may offer some reason to declare the marriage invalid if this problem existed at the time of the wedding. If not, then, the abused party should offer up his or her sufferings with the sufferings of Christ, and, if necessary, seek a temporary separation in a situation of physical danger. This heavy cross will be difficult, but it can be the path to eternal life.

Question #96

"Is everything we do a sin?" John H., 14

A. Certainly not. Only actions that are wrong, understood to be wrong, and then freely chosen are considered sins (CCC 386–87). Unless we have given the matter sufficient reflection and full consent of our will, we are not necessarily culpable (blameworthy), even if what we do is wrong in itself (CCC 1862).

God created us with free will (Sir 15:14–16; CCC 1730). Because of original sin we have an *inclination* toward sin, but we are not absolutely drawn to it, as a powerful magnet is drawn to metal (Rom 7:14–25). Nor are we ever forced into sin by Satan (CCC 1874). Sin is ultimately our choice (Sir 15:17). By relying on God's grace and practicing the virtues, we can avoid sin and lead a virtuous life (Rom 8:1–6).

Learning more about your faith (including the Commandments and Beatitudes), participating at Mass, and reading the Bible will help you develop a deeper understanding of what sin is and is not.

Question #97

"What does the Catholic Church consider a sin?"
Bob K., 15

A. The word *sin* is used in several different senses. The main definition refers to a thought, word, action, or omission contrary to God's moral law (Jas 4:17; CCC 1849–50). It amounts to saying "no" to God. It is a great evil because it deprives God of the honor due Him and the respect His laws require (Jer 2:20–22).

The Church speaks of original sin and actual sin. Original sin is not, strictly speaking, *sin*—at least not for us (CCC 404). It is the loss of the grace human beings would have if our original parents not sinned against God (Rom 5:12–17). It is the hole in our soul where the supernatural life of God is supposed to be. It is not so much a thing as the *lack* of something. Because of original sin, we inherit death, a darkened intellect, a weakened will to resist evil and corruptibility, including vulnerability to sickness and old age (Gn 2:16–17; CCC 405).

Actual sin, on the other hand, refers to sin we actually commit. Specific sins are listed in the Ten Commandments (Ex 20:1–17). Although each commandment addresses a specific sin, there are related sins under each of the ten. For example, the fifth commandment is "You shall not kill." In addition to the obvious prohibition against murder, this also prohibits things like revenge, reckless driving, giving bad example by your actions, drunkenness, and sins against human life.

Another example is the seventh commandment, "You shall not steal." In addition to taking money from people without their knowing it, this commandment also prohibits things like accepting bribes, cheating on your taxes, and damaging someone's property.

The more you learn the faith, the more you will come to see what is and is not sinful. Also, the more you go to confession, the more sensitive your soul becomes to right and wrong. I recommend reading the Beatitudes (Mt 5:1–12). You may also want to look at the examination of conscience at the end of this book.

Question #98

"What are mortal sins and what makes them different from venial sins?" Jared K., 15

A. A *mortal sin* is a serious offense against God that deprives the soul of sanctifying grace, which is necessary for salvation (1 Jn 5:16; CCC 1874). Mortal sin also takes away all merit of any good actions done while we are in mortal sin. We are separated from God and cannot "earn" our way back to grace by putting Him in our debt. We must instead *receive* His grace. This grace can be restored once we are reconciled to God by perfect contrition (in an emergency situation) and in the sacrament of reconciliation (normally).

A sin is mortal when it involves a serious matter (such as one of the Commandments [CCC 1858]), when we sufficiently reflect on its seriousness, and when we give the full consent of our wills in choosing to do it anyway. With mortal sin we lose the virtue of charity (love). We may retain the other two theological virtues of faith and hope, but these are not sufficient by themselves for salvation.

Mortal sins are like the nails that were driven into Jesus' hands and feet. It is precisely because of these sins (past, present, and future) that He died on the cross.

A venial sin is a less serious offense against God that does not cause us to lose sanctifying grace (1 Jn 5:17; CCC 1863). Strictly speaking, we do not have to go to confession for venial sins, although it is certainly helpful to our spiritual development to confess them when we think of them. A sin is venial when it is not seriously wrong or, if seriously wrong, it is done with less than full knowledge or full consent. Venial sin harms us by making us less fervent in serving God (CCC 1862).

If mortal sin is death to the soul, then venial sin should be considered a wound to the soul. If left unattended, venial sin can weaken us and make us susceptible to more serious sins.

Question #99

"What kind of sins prevent you from entering the gates of heaven?" Clare H., 14

A. Any mortal sins that a person does not repent of before death will keep him from heaven (1 Cor 6:9–10; CCC 874). By committing a mortal sin we reject God's love or truth by choosing something incompatible with the love of God (Gal 5:19–21; CCC 1857).

Since heaven is the eternal presence of God and hell the eternal absence of God, the person who sins mortally and dies alienated from God will get what he wants—an eternity without God. But it is to that person's everlasting sorrow.

Question #100

"If someone tells you something is a sin and you disagree with it, is it a sin?" Katie V., 14

A. It depends on who the "someone" is. If God says something is a sin, it is a sin. If the Magisterium of the Church (the pope and the other bishops united with him) teach something is contrary to God's law, then it is a sin. This is because Jesus promised the Magisterium special guidance to teach about matters of right and wrong without error (Mt 16:18, 28:20; Mk 16:16; Lk 10:16; 1 Tm 3:15; CCC 171, 553). Otherwise, just because someone says something is wrong does not make it so, although we should be willing to consider the advice of wiser men and women, especially parents, in such matters (1 Thess 5:12–13). Likewise, just because somebody says an act is OK (even if he is a priest or a theologian), it is not necessarily so. Check the teaching of the Church in the *Catechism* to find out what the Church's teaching is whenever you have a question or if you are not sure.

A real danger today is to think sin is merely a matter of opinion. It is not. If something is a sin, it is a sin regardless of what you or I think about it. True, if we are in genuine ignorance (CCC 1860), we may not be held accountable for a sinful action. But that does not change whether a thing is right or wrong before God. And sometimes, even if we do not know something is a sin, we can still suffer the consequences of a bad choice. A drug abuser will still suffer the physical consequences of his action, whether or not he sincerely believes drug abuse is morally acceptable.

What is really important is the correct formation of our conscience (CCC 1783). Conscience is the ability to apply our knowledge of moral principles to a particular situation (CCC 1778). We should always strive to learn more of the Church's teachings on moral issues so that our consciences are formed in light of what God has revealed (CCC 1785). It is only then that we will be able to make good, moral choices and thereby live holy, joyful, and spiritually-fruitful lives.

Question #101

"How can anyone be sinless?" Thang P., 19

A. No one can be sinless on his or her own. Only God can enable a person to remain free of sin (Phil 4:13). Through no merits of her own, the Blessed Virgin Mary was conceived without original sin by a special grace from God. This is called the Immaculate Conception (CCC 491, 508).

Mary was also preserved from personal sin throughout her life by divine grace. Otherwise, she would have been a sinner like the rest of us. This is why she called God her Savior (Lk 1:47). God saved her from the reality and effects of original sin by applying the merits of Christ's death on the cross *in advance*.

Question #102

"How good do you have to be to go to heaven?" Katie V., 14

A. You cannot be good enough on your own to deserve to go to heaven (Rom 3:23; CCC 2809). The Bible and the Catholic Church teach that a person cannot, strictly speaking, *earn* his or her way into heaven (Rom 3:20). Salvation is the free gift of God through Jesus Christ (Eph 2:8–9; Rom 3:24–25, 6:23; CCC 161, 169). But we must accept and freely cooperate with this gift (Phil 2:12–13; Gal 5:6; CCC 1949). God's grace can transform us so we can live holy lives and receive heaven as the "reward" for our faithfulness to Him (2 Cor 5:17).

Salvation means being in proper relationship with God— believing, trusting, and loving God, giving ourselves to Him wholly and freely. Baptism puts us in that relationship by communicating to us the forgiveness of Christ and the grace of being a son or daughter of God (Jn 3:5; 1 Pt 3:21–22; CCC 1999).

However, just because we have been baptized does not guarantee we will go to heaven. We can alienate ourselves from God if we willingly disobey God's law and turn our backs on Him through mortal sin (Rom 11:22; CCC 1874). Even so, God is always willing to forgive us, especially through the sacrament of reconciliation, where Christ cleanses us from our sins and reconciles us to Himself.

Question #103

"Should we do things to be saved or because we are saved?" Matthew S., 16

A. First, let us be clear on how we are saved. We are saved by grace through faith in Christ (Eph 2:8–9; CCC 161), not by our own efforts. In this sense, works *can't* save us. But we must cooperate with grace; faith must be completed by our love and obedience in order to be living, saving faith (Gal 5:6; Rom 1:8; Jas 2:8–26). Here, works of Christian obedience, motivated by the love of God and neighbor, come into play. Without such works, our faith is dead and cannot save us (CCC 162).

So our cooperation—our "work" in a very limited sense—is necessary for salvation. Yet even our cooperation is a matter of grace. As St. Paul wrote, "Work out your salvation with fear and trembling, for God is at work in you, *both to will and to work for His good pleasure*" (Phil 2:12–13, my emphasis). Even when we cooperate with God by doing good, it is God who is inspiring, enabling, and moving us to do so (Phil 4:13). Our part is to say "yes" and to love God with our whole heart, mind, and strength by active obedience.

One thing to keep in mind: Being saved is more than a "one-time event." It is a process. There are "three tenses" to salvation. If someone asks, "Are you saved?" you should answer: "I *have been* saved from my sins through Christ's death and resurrection. I *am being* saved as I cooperate with God's grace. And I *will be* saved so long as I do not reject God's love and I die in His friendship (that is, in a state of grace)." Salvation is a past, present, and future reality.

Question #104

"Could it be possible for a lot of Mormons, Jews, and Protestants who are not of the true faith to go to heaven if they have a strong faith?" Ed H., 18

A. Yes, but that does not mean everything about these faiths is correct. There are elements of truth in them, however, which a person invincibly ignorant of the Catholic Church might follow in good faith (CCC 847).

Someone might be saved despite these errors because of the power of the truth they do have and the grace of God with which they freely cooperate. If a person, moved by grace, remains faithful to the truth *as he understands it*, he could be considered an "unconscious Catholic" and be saved (Rom 2:13–16; CCC 1777).

Although someone might be saved under these circumstances, it is better to have the fullness of truth than merely part of the truth mixed with error. Some errors are so serious that they can jeopardize one's salvation if they are believed and lived (Jn 14:6; CCC 830). It is better to have the fullness of the means of salvation, such as the sacraments and the teaching authority of the Magisterium. This is one reason why we need to carry the Catholic message to the whole world.

Question #105

"If you sin, can you still get into heaven?"
Juleane S., 15

A. I hope so! Otherwise you and I almost certainly would not get there. In fact, nobody but Jesus and the Virgin Mary would be there.

The only way sin can keep us out of heaven is if we die unrepentant of mortal sin (Gal 5:19–21; CCC 1874). We have already considered why this is so in a previous question, but keep in mind the fact that to sin mortally is to reject God or to choose something incompatible with God's love. If we reject God in this way and die unrepentant, how can we expect to be with Him forever in heaven?

The Bible reminds us that if we do sin, God is eager to forgive us (Ez 33:14–16; Hos 14:3–5). But this requires repentance—being sorry for our sin and intending not to do it again—and turning back to God (Lk 13:3; Acts 3:19; CCC 1422). The sacrament of reconciliation is the normal way for Catholics to repent and receive forgiveness of sins after baptism (Jas 5:16).

Question #106

"Can you enter heaven without being baptized?"
Claire H., 14

A. Baptism is the sacrament by which we are first united to Christ, our sins are washed away, and we receive His new life of grace and become sons and daughters of God (Acts 2:38, 11:16; CCC 1213). It is the entry into the community of God's people, the Church. Consequently, it is necessary for salvation (Jn 3:3–5; CCC 1257). The person who knowingly and willingly refuses baptism cannot be saved.

Does that mean all unbaptized persons will be lost? No, for the Church also teaches the reality of a "baptism of desire," by which a person who explicitly or implicitly desires baptism—but is incapable of receiving it before death—can be saved (CCC 1281). This was the case, for instance, with the "good thief" who was crucified with Christ (Lk 23:40-43).

There is also a "baptism of blood," in which those who die for their faith in Christ without having been baptized receive the fruits of the baptism without receiving the sacrament itself (CCC 1258). Such was the case of the Holy Innocents, who the Church recognizes as martyrs for the faith.

Question #107

"If you believe in the Lord and love Him, will you have eternal life and get to heaven?" Genny C., 19

A. Yes. Of course, our belief must be more than an intellectual acceptance of certain ideas, and our love must be more than warm feelings. Faith that just says "yes" to a bunch of religious ideas cannot save; that "faith" is dead without love (Jas 2:14–16; 1 Cor 13:2; CCC 1826).

To be saved we must believe what God says, and we must love Him above all things for His own sake and everything else for love of Him (Heb 11:6). Practically speaking, that means keeping His commandments (CCC 1824). We cannot just give God "lip service"—that is, we say we will obey but then do what we want. "If you love Me," Jesus said, "you will keep My Commandments" (Jn 14:15). Needless to say, all of this we accomplish by His grace, not by our own power (Phil 2:13; 4:13; CCC 273, 308).

Question #108

"What does the Catholic Church teach about what our bodies will be like in heaven?" Jesse G., 13

A. We are told in Scripture and in Sacred Tradition that our bodies will be perfected (1 Cor 15:40–58; Phil 3:21). Theologians have suggested four characteristics that best describe what they will be like in heaven: impassable, subtle, agile, and possessing clarity.

Our glorified bodies will be *impassable*. They will experience no pain, suffering, weariness, hunger or thirst. Scripture says "[God] will wipe away every tear from their eyes, for the former things have passed away" (Rv 21:4).

We will also have the gift of *subtlety*. We will have a human body with the characteristics of a spirit. Just as Christ could walk through walls after His resurrection (Jn 20:19–20), it follows that we should be able to walk through walls. God will assimilate the characteristics of a spirit to the body without destroying the body's material characteristics.

We will also possess the gift of *agility*, which means we will not be subject to the forces of nature as we were on earth. Our playground will not be limited to the small area we can presently cover with our human powers. Rather, the farthest reaches of the universe will be accessible with the swiftness of a thought. Our bodies will also respond to the saintly direction of the soul, whereas on earth they fought against the good intentions of the will.

Finally, our bodies will have *clarity* (1 Cor 13:12) in thought and appearance. We will have glorified bodies without the ailments and infirmities of our earthly bodies. Amputations will be mended. Those who are blind will gain sight. Our immortal souls will have a more glorious home in our new bodies (CCC 1042).

For more information, you can read a variety of good books, both ancient and modern, on this subject. Peter Kreeft's *Heaven* (Ignatius Press) gives a modern presentation, as does C.S. Lewis in his *The Great Divorce* (which is not about divorce at all—it is about human choice and eternity).

Question #109

"Why are people afraid of death?" Nathan T., 15

A. There are probably several reasons. Some people have difficulty believing that if they love God and serve Him on earth He will embrace them at the time of death. Also, there is a natural fear of the unknown, even if you have faith. In addition, almost every death scene we see in the movies and on television is not a pleasant experience.

If we were to continually see the joyful faces of the canonized saints at the time of their death, our fear of death would greatly decrease, if not disappear.

It would be a good practice to meditate on the joy of seeing God at the time of your death (2 Tm 4:6–8). Scripture says, "For as a man [thinks] ... so is he" (Prv 23:7). If we think and pray about what a joyful experience heaven will be, God may give us the grace to firmly believe it. You should also develop a devotion to St. Joseph, who is the patron of a happy death.

Question #110

"Does heaven really exist?" Colin S., 14

A. Absolutely. Heaven is the ultimate and final reality for those who die in God's friendship (Is 65:17–19; 2 Thess 1:6–7; CCC 1023–24).

Because we get distracted with the good attractions of this world (entertainment, dating, fancy cars, delicious food, and so on), we often forget or even doubt the ultimate good—heaven (Mt 6:19–21). As Catholic apologist Scott

Hahn has said, "If we fill up on the hors d'oeuvres (appetizers) of life, we will not desire the heavenly banquet."

There are approximately eight hundred verses in the Bible that mention heaven. The testimony of the Word of God bears witness to its existence.

Question #111

"What is heaven?" Clark K., 14

A. The *Catechism of the Catholic Church* says that heaven is the kingdom of God, which was opened for us by the merits of Christ's death on the cross. Heaven is the place of perfect happiness, where the souls of the just see the face of God even before the resurrection of their bodies. Heaven is the eternal community of love with the Father, Son, and Holy Spirit, Mary and the angels, and all the saints (CCC 1023–1029).

Question #112

"What is heaven like?" Robert V., 15

A. Did you ever see something so beautiful that it took your breath away? After a few moments, your appreciation for this beauty fades. Well, the beatific vision (that is, the vision of God in heaven) will be like that first "awe-filled" breath (1 Jn 3:2; 2 Cor 3:18). But this breath will never end.

When people see something delightful, they occasionally burst into tears of joy. The joy is so intense that tears are the only appropriate response. This is what the beatific vision will be like. Our hearts will be so filled with God's love that they will want to burst with joy.

In heaven, not only will every wish be satisfied, but every wish will be anticipated by God. We will not even have to wish for anything (Is 35:5–10); it will already have been given to us. In fact, we will be incapable of wishing for more than we already have—because we will have God.

I can guarantee if you read good Catholic books on heaven, such as Peter Kreeft's *Everything You Ever Wanted to Know About Heaven* (Ignatius Press), and think about heaven often, you will grow in love and desire for it. When you desire something, you work toward it. Scripture supports this. Jesus said, "where your treasure is, there your heart will be" (Mt 6:21). There is no better goal to work toward than heaven.

Question #113

"Can you see things in heaven?" Robert V., 15

A. Yes, and there seems to be two different types of sight in heaven: the "sight" of the mind and soul, and actual physical sight.

We will see God "face-to-face" (1 Cor 13:12; Rv 22:3–4; 1 Jn 3:2; CCC 1023). However, this sight will be different from the sight experienced with our material bodies.

 If I ask you, "Do you see what I mean?" you are really "seeing" with your mind. This is similar to how we will know God, because God the Father does not have a body (Jn 4:24; CCC 370). We will experience God even more closely than we experience our own thoughts. We will know God in a much more direct way than the way we experience things here on earth with our senses.

We will experience God without having anything block the experience (Rv 7:9, 15). Even thoughts in our minds are "blocks" to "the real thing," because they are simply mental representations.

The second type of sight is the physical sight we experience on earth. At the end of time, after the general resurrection, we will literally see Jesus, Mary, and the saints, and our bodies will be rejoined to our souls. However, our "sight" will be different from our current experience because we will see God in all the creatures we gaze upon (1 Cor 15:41–44; CCC 1052, 1053). And because God wants all of us to be happy in heaven, we will surely see everything necessary for our happiness (Ps 36:8–10).

Based on the doctrine of the Communion of the Saints, we also believe the saints in heaven do have some knowledge of those on earth (Rv 6:9–10; Heb 12:1). We will know and understand the human experience much more deeply than we do now.

Question #114

"Are there different levels of heaven?"
Melissa D., 15

A. The Catholic Church teaches there are different levels of joy in heaven because there are different levels of reward (Mt 20:21; Jn 14:1–3; Rom 2:6–7). This difference, though, does not cause any jealousy or distance between the saints, because all are perfected in charity and perfectly happy in the presence of God.

Here is a frequently used analogy: Imagine your soul is like a glass. In heaven, some people will have a large "glass"; others will have a small "glass." Those with large glasses can have more of God's love poured into them (that is, poured into their soul) because they loved more perfectly on earth. They prepared their soul to receive more of God. The person with a smaller "glass" can hold less of God's love but will still be completely filled with Him. Yet, he or she will want for nothing and will not be jealous of those who receive more of God's love.

Here is another analogy: Think of an athlete who, after years of vigorous aerobic training, has developed a greater lung capacity than an inactive person. This athlete can absorb more oxygen into his or her bloodstream. Think of the oxygen in this example as grace. If we "train" our hearts by exercising them in love and grace, we will have a greater capacity to "take in" God's grace.

Question #115

"What is hell?" Philip S., 14

A. Hell is the eternal separation from God and the blessed (CCC 1033). Hell is the place where the souls (and ultimately, the bodies) of unrepentant sinners go for all eternity. Hell was originally created for Satan and the other fallen angels who rebelled against God at the beginning of time. However, with the fall of man through original sin, people too can now go to hell as punishment for unrepented sins against God.

According to the *Catechism*, hell is "reserved for those who to the end of their lives refuse to believe and be converted" (CCC 1034). It is for those who die in a state of mortal sin and who intentionally do not repent before death. References in the Bible to hell as a punishment for sin include Isaiah 3:11, Romans 2:5–8, and 1 Corinthians 6:9–10.

Hell is also referred to as "Gehenna" (Mk 9:43–47; Mt 5:22). It has been described as a prison (Job 38:17); a place of torment and misery (Dn 12:2; Mt 8:11–12; Lk 13:24–28); a pit (Ps 88; Job 33; Job 26:5–6; 2 Pt 2:4); a place of darkness (Ps 88:7; Jude 13); an unquenchable fire where the worm does not die (Is 66:24); and a lake of fire (Rv 19:20). Human images used to describe hell include wailing, gnashing of teeth, pain, stench, unquenchable thirst, binding chains, and incredible darkness. We can conclude, then, that there is only hate in hell, especially hate for God.

Few doctrines in Scripture are more frequently affirmed than hell; there are a dozen such references from Jesus Himself. Hell is a necessary requirement of God's justice.

The existence of hell is a dogma of the Faith that Catholics are required to believe (CCC 1035).

Question #116

"What kind of pain or punishment do you endure in hell?" Clare H., 14

A. Hell is the exclusion from our majestic God's presence (Mt 5:20, 7:21–23; 1 Cor 6:9–10; Gal 5:19–21; 2 Thess 1:9; CCC 1035). This is the primary pain of hell.

Human beings were made for union with God and are intended to be with Him for all eternity (Heb 11:13–16; CCC 1). Some theologians speculate that a person in hell will contemplate his intended destiny with God and how his selfishness kept him from this. He will see the emptiness of his excessive self-love and will have a vivid knowledge of his offenses. He will see the many gifts God offered and remember how he rejected them.

Is the "fire" of hell literal or merely symbolic of severe punishment? Theologians differ on this point. Certainly, hellfire is different in many respects from the ordinary fire we know (Mt 25:30). Scripture speaks of hell as the "outer darkness," whereas the fire we experience on earth creates light. Also, the fire of hell is perpetual and capable of punishing spiritual beings—again, something very different from earthly fire (Rv 14:11).

We do not know exactly what hellfire will be like. However, whatever it is like, the primary effect will be a spiritual torture of our souls, knowing we shall never be with God.

We know from Scripture that God is love (1 Jn 4:8). Even though those in hell are cut off from the source of love (God), they will understand the goodness of God and despise it.

At the same time, the incompleteness they will feel because they will not have union with God will be a never-ending frustration and torment.

Question #117

"How could there be a place like hell if Jesus loves people unconditionally?" Jennifer N., 17

A. While it is absolutely true that Jesus loves all people unconditionally, this does not mean that Jesus saves people unconditionally.

We humans were created with the tremendous gift of free will. We can freely choose God or reject Him. He did not make us robots programmed to obey Him. He created us in His image and likeness (which necessarily includes free will), and this creation was an act of love (Gn 1:27; CCC 355, 374, 380). Now with free will comes the possibility that we will freely choose to reject God. What God desires, however, is our freely-given love and obedience (CCC 358). He constantly invites us to love Him, but he will not (indeed, cannot) force us (CCC 1864). There is no such thing as "forced love." For love to actually be love, it must be freely given.

Here are seven reasons why a place like hell is reasonable to believe in and, despite its horror, is still compatible with God's love:

1. *What else can God do with a man who does not love Him?* If a man dies loving himself more than God, what can God do with him? He has to let him go to the place of his own choosing. He cannot take him to heaven and force him to love Him, for that would involve an inconceivably close union with God, whom the man hates. Loving God and being close to Him would be a torment to the man, who really loves himself most of all. It is impossible for a man to reject God and possess Him at the same time.

2. *Jesus (and the Father) would not lie* (Rom 3:4; Ps 119:89; CCC 2465–66). God the Father and the Son reveal many times in Scripture that hell is real. How then could God say, "I was only kidding"? God does not kid about something as serious as hell. Therefore, it must be true.

3. *God is love* and *justice* (1 Jn 4:8; Rv 16:5–7). God is not 51 percent love and 49 percent justice or vice versa. God is 100 percent love and 100 percent justice at the same time. By His very nature (that is, perfection), God is incapable of an injustice. Therefore, eternal punishment must be just.

Our free will is a gift that is in accord with our dignity as human beings (CCC 1730). It would be an injustice for God to force us to love Him because this would go against our nature as humans. It would not offer the challenge or choice that our intellects and free will deserve. It would be an injustice for Him *not* to allow us to use our free will to choose or reject Him (CCC 1732). Therefore, hell can actually be an argument *for* the justice of God.

4. *Because the offense is so serious, the punishment must be serious.* If a person assaults another person, he may go to prison for a year. If he assaults the mayor, he will go to prison for a longer time. If he assaults the president of the United States, he will go for an even longer time. And if he assaults the eternal God, by rejecting Him and His laws, it is not unreasonable to think he should go to "prison" for all eternity (CCC 1874). Why? The penalty is measured by the gravity of the offense and the importance of the person assaulted (Lk 12:47–48; CCC 1864). Rejecting an infinite God (and not repenting) merits an infinite punishment.

5. *God does not condemn people to hell. They condemn themselves.* God simply allows their condemnation. He knows that because the person rejected Him, the condemnation is just (Col 3:25; 1 Pt 4:18). God has

given us every possible aid to avoid hell. He gave His only Son (Jn 3:16). He gave the Church and the pope to teach us (Mt 16:18–19; 1 Tm 3:15). He gave us the Bible as written documentation of His truth (2 Tim 3:14–17). He gave us the Eucharist to nourish us spiritually (Jn 6:48–58). He gave us confession to heal us spiritually (Jn 20:21–23). He even gave us the anointing of the sick for those who are close to death (Jas 5:14–16). He gave us miracles to help us believe (Jn 2:1–11; Mt 15:32–38). Yet, people still reject Him (Jn 6:60–66). Some could not care less about Him or His laws. What is God to do with them without offending their human dignity and free will?

6. *Because people would live more sinful lives if there were not the threat of hell.* The possibility of spending eternity in hell is a great deterrent for bad behavior (Mk 9:42–48). Hell is an "emergency brake" against a life of sin.

Time has proven that, because of our sinful nature and love of self, too many people choose to live for themselves instead of God. *And this is in a world that mostly believes that hell exists.* Can you imagine what life would be like if Christianity taught that there was a second chance after this life? Many people would act much differently. Many would say, "I'm going to go wild here on earth because I plan to repent in the next life." We would have chaos. We would have much more abortion, homicide, premarital sex, and other evils.

7. *If punishment on earth is OK, why not in the afterlife?* If we reject the idea of eternal punishment, why not reject temporal (earthly) punishment? Why

have prisons? Why have traffic tickets for speeding violations? Why have penalties for crimes here on earth if we are not prepared to have penalties for crimes committed against the One who made the earth? Penalties for crimes are necessary in order to maintain earthly justice and order. Likewise, penalties for crimes against God are necessary in order to maintain justice and order in the spiritual realm.

It is important to remember that you are in *no danger of hell* if you simply love God and live this love by staying faithful to His laws (Rom 10:10–13). God will help us. And, if you fall into sin, get back up and be reconciled through the sacrament of reconciliation (Jn 20:21–23). God does not take pleasure in allowing people to go to hell. Nor should we take pleasure in the thought of anybody doing so, or worse still, in the hope that our enemy will. This would be a warped view of justice. We should want all to be saved. We should pray as we were instructed to by Our Lady at Fatima, "Lead all souls to heaven, especially those in most need of Thy mercy."

Question #118

"What is purgatory? Megann R., 15

A. Purgatory is the state of purification that some souls must undergo before experiencing the Beatific Vision, the vision of God. Purgatory is an infallible dogma of the faith (CCC 1030).

Purgatory is for people who are destined for heaven but have venial sins or the effects of forgiven mortal sins on their souls (Mt 5:26; CCC 1031). Because "nothing unclean shall enter" into heaven (Rv 21:27), God has established a place of final purification—purgatory. Purgatory is not a "second chance." If one dies in mortal sin, one goes directly to hell (CCC 1874). If one dies in a state of grace and has completely formed his will and love of God to a state of perfection, one will go straight to heaven.

When we are judged immediately after death (Heb 9:27; 2 Cor 5:10), we will know the true state of our souls and our life's work as never before. If we are saved but are still attached to the vestiges (remnants) of sin, we will not only see the justice and logic of purgatory but will actually *want* to go there. As C.S. Lewis once wrote, "Our souls *demand* purgatory, don't they?" (See his book *The Joyful Christian*.) Before we come into the presence of an all-holy, perfect God, we will need and want to be purified of anything unholy or imperfect that remains.

When we sin, we love ourselves more than God and His laws. This is disordered love. This sin is like the impurities found in newly mined gold. To make the gold perfect, we need to put it through fire. The fire "sweats out" the impurities. This is analogous to the purification process in purgatory (1 Cor 3:12–13).

There is a common objection, directed at the Church by some Protestants, that the doctrine of purgatory takes away from the work of Jesus on the cross at Calvary and is therefore unbiblical. This is not true. Purgatory is an *application* of the cross. Jesus' death is so powerful that it can actually purify us in the afterlife. The souls in purgatory are cleansed of their sin precisely because of the sufferings of Christ on the cross.

Question #119

"What kind of pain or punishment do people endure in purgatory?" Clare H., 14

A. There are two primary things going on at the same time in purgatory: pain and joy. The souls there have the pain of sadness because they are not with God and yet are yearning for Him. They have joy because they know they are saved and will soon be with Him. Let me address both aspects in greater detail.

The pains in purgatory have often been referred to in terms of "fire." This description is rooted in certain biblical texts, including 1 Corinthians 3:15. Others have said the fire is merely a metaphor for the intense pain people experience in their yearning for God. The Church has not defined whether fire is a part of purgatory.

You may have heard the phrase "burning love" (Heb 12:29). This is the feeling in purgatory. When you love someone, you want to be with him or her. If you cannot, there is pain. The greater the unfulfilled desire, the greater the pain.

God is the ultimate good. Once we are saved, every fiber of our being will long for the vision of the Father. The degree of pain in purgatory is in direct proportion to one's realization of the greatness of God and the frustration of having rejected His graces during our earthly life.

Regarding the joys of purgatory, consider this story: Imagine you have grown to love someone from a foreign country very deeply. After fifty years of writing letters to each other, you have come to know him or her, but you have never met this person. Your love has grown deeper each week because of the intimacy you have both experienced from the letters. You then receive a train ticket to visit your pen pal. As the train you are on nears the station, your excitement builds. You are about to meet your love after fifty years of friendship! You are incredibly excited about this face-to-face visit.

This is similar to the joy of purgatory. A person's love is being perfected in purgatory, and his or her burning desire to see God is increasing by the second. The pain of this love is greater than any pain ever experienced because of not being with God, but the joy in knowing one will soon be with Him for all eternity makes the suffering worth it.

Question #120

"How can I persuade my Protestant friends that purgatory exists?" Jesse G., 13

A. First find out what they believe purgatory is and why they object to it. Chances are they misunderstand the doctrine.

Then explain how both you and your friends agree that Jesus wants us to be holy. Remind your friends that Jesus said, "So be perfect, just as your heavenly Father is perfect" (Mt 5:48). Point out that Hebrews 12:14 instructs us to strive "for that holiness without which no one will see the Lord," and Revelation 21:27 declares that "nothing unclean will enter heaven."

Explain that while Jesus took away our sins on the cross, we must still be sanctified (made holy) by the Holy Spirit. If we are not perfectly sanctified in this life, then we must be in the next in order to enter heaven. God disciplines those he accepts as His children (Heb 12:5-11).

The Old and New Testaments support belief in purgatory. Although the word "purgatory" is not mentioned by name, the *truth* of purgatory is there. (By the way, the words *trinity* and *incarnation* are not explicitly used in the Bible either, but the realities they express certainly are.) In the second book of Maccabees, we read: "It is a holy and wholesome thought to pray for the dead that they might be loosed from their sins" (2 Mc 12:46). The early Protestants did not include 2 Maccabees in their version of the Bible because they could not reconcile what it taught with their rejection of purgatory. In doing so, they rejected fifteen hundred years of unbroken Christian tradition.

In the New Testament we read that some will be saved, "but only as through fire" (1 Cor 3:15). We also read, "The judge will hand you over to the guard, and you will be thrown into prison. Amen, I say to you, you will not be released until you have paid the last penny" (Mt 5:25–26). These passages do not fit very well with the biblical teaching on hell, from which nobody is ever released. They do, however, fit well with the traditional understanding of purgatory.

Question #121

"Can we actually help those in purgatory get out by our prayers?" Ed H., 18

A. Yes. The members of the body of Christ are connected to each other (1 Cor 12:14–26). The Church refers to three types of Christians: the Church Militant (those on earth), the Church Triumphant (those in heaven), and the Church Suffering (those in purgatory). We are all part of the same mystical body of Christ, whether in heaven, on earth, or in purgatory (CCC 954).

The Bible exhorts us to pray for one another (1 Tm 2:1–4; 2 Mc 12:46). This prayer includes *all* members of the body, especially those in need. Those in purgatory are in special need because they cannot help themselves (CCC 958).

Our prayers, especially the Mass, relieve the suffering of the holy souls in purgatory (Jn 5:16; CCC 1032). These souls are eternally grateful for our prayers and will remember us when they get to heaven (Rv 6:9–10). If we go to purgatory, they will surely pray for us. Praying for the dead is an obligation for Catholics, so keep up this good and holy practice.

Question #122

"What are the 'end times'?" Christopher H., 19

A. The "end times" are often considered the final period of human history, prior to the second coming of Christ. The Bible also speaks of the "last days."

Are we living in the "last days"? Yes, and we have been for nearly two thousand years (Acts 2:17; CCC 670). The "last days" began with the death, resurrection, and ascension of Christ and the outpouring of the Spirit on Pentecost (CCC 670).

The Scriptures (and even some approved apparitions) see the end times as a period of tribulation, chastisement, purification, and eventual peace right before Jesus' actual return (CCC 675).

For a concise overview of popular "end times" speculation and for the traditional Christian teaching on *eschatology* (Greek for the study of the "last things"), read *The Rapture Trap* by Paul Thigpen (Ascension Press).

Question #123

"When do you think the world will end?"
Jessica C., 13

A. Scripture says that no one except the Father knows the time when the end will come (Mt 24:36; CCC 673). Thank goodness I do not know the date because that would cause me and anyone I would tell tremendous emotional stress.

The only thing we do know for sure is that it will happen at the appropriate time. It will happen when some goal of all mankind has been achieved, according to Catholic apologist Frank Sheed in his book *Theology for Beginners*. Sheed proposes it would be silly to think that God will suddenly lose patience with wayward mankind. When God created the world, He knew when it would end.

The end will come when all who are to be incorporated into the Church are incorporated into it. The Church Militant will have fulfilled its purpose, which is the delivering of the Good News to all peoples and nations (Mt 28:19).

Question #124

"Will there be signs to tell us the world is going to end?" Erinn T., 16

A. Scripture says there will be some signs we can look for, including a great apostasy (or "falling away") from the Catholic Church (2 Thess 2:1-4), and the arrival of the Antichrist, who will be a man, not a demon (Dn 11; CCC 675).

This Antichrist will be someone who is aided by Satan (Rv 13:11–18). As Christ had the prophet John the Baptist as His herald, the Antichrist will have the "false prophet" as his herald (Rv 16:13–14, 19:20; CCC 676). Scripture also mentions a mass conversion of the Jewish people after they recognize Jesus as the Messiah for whom they waited (Rom 11:26).

Question #125

"What Catholic miracles have occurred?"
Colin S., 14

A. They are too numerous to count. To begin, all miracles of Jesus are considered Catholic miracles, because He is the founder of our faith. These miracles included the multiplication of the loaves, the turning of water into wine at the wedding feast at Cana, the raising of Lazarus from the dead, and Jesus' own Resurrection (Mk 6:34–44; Jn 2:1–11, 11:1–44; Lk 24:36–49). Jesus gave sight to the blind and hearing to the deaf. He cured lepers and cripples. The Gospels are full of His miracles.

There have been many miracles since Jesus ascended into heaven, such as miracles of healing. The bodies of dead saints have been found incorrupt hundreds of years after their deaths. We have Eucharistic miracles in which the Body of Jesus (formerly the bread) and the Blood of Jesus (formerly the wine) have actually turned to visible flesh and blood. These can be seen today. (For more information on such miracles, see the powerful books *Eucharistic Miracles* and *The Incorruptables*, both published by TAN Books.)

Another well-known miracle we can still see today is that of the *tilma* (or cloak) that St. Juan Diego was wearing when he saw the apparition of Our Lady in Guadalupe, Mexico. It bears a miraculous image of Our Lady. The tilma itself should have disintegrated by now, since it is over 450 years old, yet it still shows little sign of age.

Science is unable to explain any of these events.

Question #126

"Can you describe the role Mary plays in the Catholic faith? I know she was chosen to be the Mother of God, but can you go into more detail?"
Vanessa C., 16

A. Mary said "yes" to God when the angel Gabriel announced to her the divine plan that she would be the Mother of the Savior (Lk 1:38; CCC 494). She was the human instrument God chose to bring about salvation. It was from her that Christ took His human nature. She is our human link to Him.

Adam and Eve's "no" to God was enough to cast all mankind into darkness and death until the coming of the Savior (Gn 3:1–19; CCC 511). This is why the Church acknowledges that Mary's "yes" cooperated with God's grace in the salvation of mankind.

Mary must be special. Out of all the billions of women in history, she was the one chosen to bear God in her womb (Lk 1:43; CCC 488). She would be the one to nurse, play with, and teach the infant Jesus, who is

God. This was a *big* task, the greatest responsibility and honor ever given to a human being.

Mary is also an intercessor for us. The first record of her intercession is at the wedding feast of Cana where she asked her Son to assist when the wine ran out (Jn 2:3–11). Jesus responded by performing His first recorded miracle. Mary continues to intercede for us each time we invoke her in prayer (CCC 969, 970).

Question #127

"How can a Catholic explain to non-Catholics how wonderful and good the Blessed Virgin Mary is, how we do not worship her but rather ask her to pray to God for us?" Kelly T., 15

A. Jesus was a good Jewish boy who kept the Commandments perfectly. The fourth commandment requires us to "Honor your father and mother" (Ex 20:12). The Hebrew word for honor also means to glorify. So, Jesus glorified His mother.

Our goal as Christians is to imitate Jesus. We, too, should "glorify" His mother (CCC 970). This is not only scriptural (Lk 1:48); it is also the command of Christ. For Mary is not just the mother of our Lord: she is our mother, too. That is why John's Gospel tells how Jesus told the "beloved disciple" to "behold your mother" and commanded her to "behold your son." That story is not just about John and Mary. Rather, John wants us to understand that we are the beloved disciple, too, and Mary is our mother.

The real question you should ask your non-Catholic friends is, "Why are you *not* giving Mary high recognition? She played a very important role in our salvation by allowing the Father to give us the Son through her." If we can honor Thomas Jefferson or a modern sports hero, why can't we honor a great saint like Mary?

Regarding the "worship" of Mary, the Catholic Church would seriously condemn such an action. Mary is a created being, whereas worship (or *latria* in Greek) is reserved for God alone (Ex 20:1–6).

Sometimes you will find older Catholic writings that do speak of "worshiping" Mary. It is important, however, to understand that "worship" is an English word that has changed in meaning over the centuries. The same time period that spoke of "worshiping" Mary also had wedding vows in which the husband and wife said to each other, "With my body, I thee worship." In short, *worship* used to mean what we now mean by *honor* or *reverence*. Today, *worship* is used to describe the honor given to God alone (though its older meaning still lingers on whenever a British citizen calls a judge "Your Worship").

The Church encourages us to give Mary the special recognition she deserves (CCC 971). We are allowed to give the saints *dulia*, which is Greek for "praise." And, we are allowed to give Mary *hyper-dulia*, which is Greek for "extra praise." Catholic teaching on Mary authentically expresses the biblical idea that Mary is "blessed among women" (Lk 1:42; CCC 148) and that "all generations" shall call her blessed (Lk 1:48; CCC 971).

Question #128

"What is the pope's role?" Michael W., 14

A. As the successor to St. Peter, the pope's role is to be an earthly father to the people of God. (The word pope means "father.") He is also the shepherd appointed by the greatest Shepherd of them all—Jesus (Jn 21:15–17). As Peter led the apostolic college, so his successor, the pope, leads the episcopal college of bishops (CCC 880). In this capacity, he confirms his brother bishops and priests in the Faith (Lk 22:32), and works with them to spread the Gospel and to pastor the flock of God (Mt 28:18–20; 1 Pt 5:1–3; CCC 882). The document *Lumen Gentium* of the Second Vatican Council (1962-1965), speaks of the pope's role as the Church's "principle of unity." This means that he has "full, supreme, and universal power over the whole Church" as the sucessor of St. Peter and head of the college of bishops (*Lumen Gentium* 22; CCC 882).

The pope protects the deposit of faith given to the Church two thousand years ago by Jesus. He does not make new doctrine, nor can he change a doctrine to mean something different from what it meant in the past (CCC 891). His role is to pass on the faith to the Church (Jude 3).

Question #129

"How does the pope get elected by the Church?" Guy C., 14

A. Upon the death of a pope, there is a traditional nine-day period of mourning. Immediately after this, the college of cardinals meets in an electoral session (or *conclave*) and chooses the man whom they believe the Holy Spirit has guided them to choose. The new pope must be named on at least two-thirds of the ballots plus one.

Shortly after the selection is made, the pope is asked by the head of the college if he accepts the nomination. If he says yes, he is then asked, "What will you be called?" The ballots are then burned. This gives us the white smoke, that is the signal to the world that a new pope has been chosen. An announcement is then made in Latin: "I bring you a message of great joy. We have a pope, [his birth name], who has chosen the name [his new name]."

For more information about the history and process of choosing a new pope, you may want to consult the booklet *When a Pope Dies* by Christopher M. Bellitto, Ph.D (Ligouri Publications). It contains many interesting facts about how papal elections have changed over the two thousand years of Church history.

Question #130

"How can the pope be totally infallible? If he is, why does he not win the lottery?" Paul K., 13

A. The pope is not "totally infallible." His infallibility extends only to matters of faith and morals, and it can operate only when he is defining something pertaining to faith or morals for the whole Church (CCC 891, 2035).

Infallibility is a special gift God gave to the Church to protect it from teaching as true what is, in fact, false (CCC 889). It is a special protection to ensure that the

Faith will not be distorted by error (Mt 16:18–19).

The pope does not have a "hotline" to God. He must get his doctrine the same way we do—he must pray and study. Infallibility means that only after he has prayed and studied, and when he defines something as part of the Catholic faith, the Holy Spirit protects what he teaches from being wrong (Lk 22:31–32). It refers to his function as official teacher, not as a private person, nor even as a private theologian. Thus, not everything the pope writes or says about the faith is to be considered infallible.

In fact, all the bishops of the Church in union with the pope share this gift. They are protected from teaching error when they meet in a council to define a matter of faith or morals, or when, scattered throughout the world, they agree on how a matter of faith or morals is to be definitively held (Mt 18:18; CCC 891).

Because it applies only to matters of faith or morals, the gift of infallibility does not mean the pope should know about the winning lottery numbers. Nor is he guaranteed to correctly predict the winner of the Super Bowl.

Also, infallibility is not inspiration. This means that the pope is not automatically given the proper words with which to teach. Infallibility is a *negative protection*. It is like a guardrail along a mountain highway. It keeps the pope from "going over the edge" into teaching error. The Holy Spirit will never allow the pope to teach as truth something that is actually false.

Sometimes infallibility is confused with "impeccability," which is the idea that the pope is sinless or cannot sin. This is not what infallibility means. A pope could live a seriously sinful life, as a few popes have, yet his teaching would still be protected by the Holy Spirit. This is the point of infallibility—to protect the Church's teaching from error. A pope may even end up in hell for living a sinful life, but his teaching would still have been protected by the Holy Spirit.

Here are the conditions necessary for infallible teaching by the pope (see CCC 891):

1. The pope makes it clear that he is exercising his supreme *ex cathedra* authority. (*Ex cathedra* is Latin for "from the chair" and refers to the pope's office as universal pastor and teacher of the faith.)

2. He is defining a matter pertaining to faith or morals.

3. The pope uses terms that make it clear he is rendering an infallible judgment.

4. He is addressing the whole Church, not just a part of it.

5. He makes it clear that his teaching binds the consciences of the faithful.

Question #131

"Why can't we eat meat on Fridays in Lent?"
Rachel P., 13

A. The Church asks us to abstain from meat as a means of "offering our bodies as a living sacrifice" in union with Christ (Rom 12:1; CCC 1434). The purpose is not to make life tough for us. The Church is truly working in our best interest and only asks us to do what is ultimately good for us.

Abstaining from meat is a part of a whole penitential approach to Friday that should be maintained throughout the year but especially in Lent. As a young person, you may not have grown up in an environment when all Fridays throughout the year were days of abstinence from meat. Yet even today we are obliged to do some form of penance *every Friday* because it is the day of Jesus' crucifixion, the ultimate sacrifice (CCC 1438).

We do penance for several reasons:

1. As a way to atone for sins of the past, both ours and others (Col 1:24).
2. To learn to master our inclinations toward sin (Jas 1:2–4).
3. To help us prepare for the spiritual feast of the resurrection of Jesus on Easter.
4. As a sign of our conversion.
5. As a way to purify our soul (CCC 2043).

The *Catechism of the Catholic Church* also says that we have Lent as a time to unite the Church with the mystery of Christ's time of temptation in the desert (CCC 540). There Christ fasted for forty days.

Mastering the little challenges in life prepares us for the big challenges (Heb 5:8; 1 Pt 4:12–13). A person who can rise to little challenges like abstaining from meat one day a week is more likely to rise to more difficult challenges.

In the United States, the rules for fasting apply on Ash Wednesday and Good Friday. On these days, we are permitted only one full meal and two small meals that together add up to no more than one full meal, and we must abstain from eating meat. Days of abstinence (such as the Fridays of Lent) simply require the avoidance of meat on those days.

Question #132

"Why do we go to church on Sunday instead of another day?" Erik L., 14

A. Saturday was the Sabbath for the Jews, but the early Catholics changed the practice to Sunday to commemorate Jesus' rising from the dead on Sunday (Acts 20:7; Rv 1:10; CCC 2042).

For the first Jewish Christians, both Saturday (the original Sabbath) and Sunday were regarded as festival days. As the number of Jewish converts to Christianity decreased, the Christian observance of Saturday as a holy day diminished.

For the gentile (that is, non-Jewish) Christians, Saturday never had any particular importance. They observed Sunday as the holy day.

There have been attempts by a few modern Protestant sects to reestablish Saturday as the day of worship. The most notable of these is the Seventh-Day Adventists. This practice has no historical basis and is contrary to the practice of the early Church (CCC 1343).

Question #133

"Where does holy water come from and what is its purpose?" Megann R., 15

Holy water is actually just ordinary water that has been blessed and to which some salt has been added. The salt signifies our future preservation from corruption. The purpose of holy water is to remind us of our baptism. It signifies that we are worthy to enter into the presence of Christ only through the grace of baptism (CCC 1668).

Question #134

"How does one become a priest?" Charles C., 13

A. First by contacting the local diocese or a religious order. The process includes some psychological evaluation to determine whether you are a good prospect for the trials and demands of ministry. This evaluation also focuses on your views, beliefs, and ability to interact socially and pastorally. Another key element is an assessment of your reasons for wanting to become a priest.

After one is accepted, the applicant receives spiritual, academic, psychological, and social guidance to prepare him for ministry. This is a rewarding (but lengthy) training process and includes a firm grounding in the doctrines of the Church. Some dioceses even require special language training. All this is to prepare the future priest for the challenges that lie ahead in his life of service to the Lord.

Naturally, each diocese has different needs so this makes identifying the exact characteristics of the desired type of priest somewhat difficult to pinpoint. Canon Law requires that a priest be at least twenty-five years old when he is ordained (Can 1031).

Question #135

"Why are priests not allowed to get married?"
Amy F., 14

A. Although the early Church allowed married clergy, the Church later came to see celibacy as a better reflection of Jesus' priesthood.

St. Paul said: "Indeed, I wish everyone to be as I am, but each has a particular gift from God. . . .Now to the unmarried and to widows I say: it is a good thing for them to remain as they are, as I do... an unmarried man is anxious about the things of the Lord, how he may please the Lord. But a married man is anxious about the things of the world, how he may please his wife, and he is divided" (1 Cor 7:7-8, 32-34).

Jesus said: "And everyone who has given up houses or brothers or sisters or father or mother or children or lands for the sake of my name will receive a hundred times more, and will inherit eternal life" (Mt 19:29).

Celibacy is a discipline, not a dogma. This means that the Church could change the rule. In fact, there are a few instances when the Church has allowed married priests, such as with some Eastern rite clergy and some Protestant ministers who converted to the faith. These, however, are the exceptions.

It is unlikely that the Church will change this discipline anytime soon because of the many positive and practical benefits of celibacy. Here are ten reasons why a celibate clergy makes good sense:

1. Celibacy leaves the priest free to more fully commit his life to the service of the Lord and the laity.

2. The Church has found it good to move priests from parish to parish every few years. There are a few reasons for this, including the desire to prevent personality cults from developing around particular priests. Such a situation can put too much focus on the priest rather than on the gospel message.

   Can you imagine how much stress it would cause a priest to have to move his wife and family each time he is assigned to a new parish? Having a celibate priesthood enables the bishop the full flexibility he needs to move priests around.

3. Celibacy enables a priest to lay his life down for his flock. Because a celibate priest does not have the obligation to care for a wife and children, he can give of himself more easily, including his own life if necessary. For example, Blessed Damien de Veuster of Belgium was able to work with lepers on the island of Molokai, Hawaii, because of the freedom he had in being a celibate minister. This work eventually led to his contracting and dying from leprosy.

4. Celibacy is a sign of contradiction and a great Christian witness to our society, which is flooded with sexually permissive messages. Celibacy surely gains the Catholic clergy a hidden respect from many people.

5. Celibacy gives the priest greater credibility when he asks the laity to make sacrifices, because the laity knows that celibacy involves sacrifice.

6. Celibacy helps the priest master his passions and also gives him more time for prayer, which is the lifeblood of any ministry.

7. Celibacy enables a priest to be more objective when counseling married couples. He does not project any personal marriage problems or biases onto the couple he is counseling.

8. In many cases, celibacy enables the priest to be a "spiritual father" to more people than he would as a married man (1 Cor 4:15).

9. Celibacy allows the Church to put the hundreds of millions of dollars it saves in priestly salaries towards the evangelization and charitable assistance of a needy world. Although priests do receive salaries, these are much lower than they would have to be if priests had families to support.

10. Celibacy is a foreshadowing that there will be no marriage in heaven (Mt 22:30).

No one is required to live a permanently celibate life (Mt 19:12). The Church says that people are free to marry. In fact, the Church glorifies the married state. Only if one wants to become a priest, brother, or religious sister does he or she have to live a celibate life. When the priesthood or religious life is chosen, it needs to be lived in the manner the Church requires.

Celibacy can be difficult, especially in this sexually permissive age. But if a priest has good seminary formation that strongly supports celibacy and if he stays close to the Lord in prayer, he will be able to turn this sacrifice into a wonderful aid to his work.

Question #136

"Can a man cease to be a priest if he gets married?"
Christopher R., 15

A. Strictly speaking, once a man is validly ordained, he remains a priest forever (Ps 110:4; Heb 5:6). He may, however, be relieved of the obligations of priestly ministry (CCC 1583). This can happen by *laicization*, whereby a priest is released from his sacred promises of celibacy and obedience by the authority of the pope. If he is a *religious* priest (that is, a priest in a religious order such as the Franciscans or Jesuits), he is released from his vows of poverty, chastity, and obedience.

Once laicized, the man still has priestly powers to forgive sins and consecrate the Eucharist, but he is forbidden to use them, except in emergency circumstances.

Question #137

"Don't you think a lot more men would become priests if they were allowed to get married?"
Brian K., 13

A. It is not at all clear that allowing a married priesthood would increase the number of priests in any significant way. A married priesthood might increase the numbers in the short-run. But the real question is this: "In the long run, would having married priests as the norm better help the Church fulfill its mission?" I have already explained the advantages of a celibate priesthood in a previous answer.

The real problem with the lower number of priestly vocations today is that many men do not have the spiritual awareness necessary to hear and answer God's call to priestly ministry (CCC 1578). Others are unwilling to make the personal sacrifices necessary to serve as priests. Ordaining married men would only mean that one less sacrifice would be required of men already disinclined to live a completely sacrificial life, which is the essence of priestly ministry. That does not seem to be a recipe for good priests (Mt 10:5–10).

And just because a man—married or unmarried—thinks he is called to priestly ministry does not mean he is—or that he has the qualifications to serve effectively as a priest. This must be discerned by Church authorities and by the man himself.

Although the Church in North America and Europe is currently experiencing a serious decrease in the number of priestly vocations, other parts of the world (especially Africa and Asia) are seeing a dramatic *increase* in vocations. I have great confidence that God will take care of His Church by calling enough men to this sacred office.

Question #138

"Why aren't women allowed to be priests?"
Megan M., 14

A.The Church's teaching about the male-only priesthood is difficult for some people today to accept. They overlook the fact that there are two crucial truths about gender, not just one. In addition to equality, *difference* must also be considered.

Jesus made the priesthood a male thing—like fatherhood. This has nothing to do with men being superior to women—they are not (CCC 1577). Men and women are equal in their human dignity; they are equally made "in the image of God." But such equality does not mean "sameness" in all respects, nor does it mean men and women must be entirely interchangeable or that they cannot have different roles in a community.

Because some women have been unjustly discriminated against in society and even by Church members, some people assume that allowing only men to be priests is an injustice. But it is not. Jesus is the One who established the priesthood, and He is the One who called only men to be priests.

People sometimes say Jesus did this because of the prevailing customs of His time. This is a very weak argument. Jesus freely broke with those customs in other instances, especially regarding women. For example, He allowed women to be among His close followers, He addressed them in public, and He upheld their rights in marriage on the same terms as men (Mt 15:21–28; Mk 10:2–12). And, of course, if he was really interested in conforming to cultural norms, he would have avoided claiming to be God and telling people they must eat his flesh and blood—both of which were radically forbidden by his culture. That He did not call any women to be priests is a clear indication He intended priestly ministry to be exclusively male (Mt 10:1–4).

Further evidence of this is found in His mother, the Blessed Virgin. As Pope John Paul II has said, "The fact that the Blessed Virgin Mary, the Mother of God and Mother of the Church, received neither the mission proper to the Apostles nor the ministerial priesthood clearly shows that the non-admission of women to priestly ordination cannot mean that women are of less dignity, nor can it be construed as discrimination against them" (*Ordinatio Sacerdotalis*, no. 3). "Rather," he writes, "it is to be seen as the faithful observance of a plan to be ascribed to the Wisdom of the Lord of the Universe."

The Church does not have the authority to change what Christ has established. Even if the pope wanted to, he could not permit women to be priests. The Church is not the pope's Church; it is Christ's Church.

Perhaps it might help to consider why the priesthood is limited to men. The Church itself has always been considered in "feminine" terms. We speak of the Church as the bride of Christ (Rv 21:9). Even the term *body of Christ* is linked to the femininity of the Church by St. Paul in Ephesians, chapter 5. There the Church is the body of Christ because she is "one flesh" or "one body" with Christ, as the wife is one flesh or one body with her husband.

Why is the Church feminine? One reason is that she receives grace from outside herself and nourishes the new life of believers within herself, as a mother nourishes her unborn children from within. This is why we sometimes speak of the Church as "Holy Mother Church."

How is this relevant to a male priesthood? The priest is a sacramental sign of Christ as Bridegroom of the Church—an inherently male identity. It is no accident that the Second Person of the Trinity became a male human being. His identity, in relation to God's people, is masculine, and the people of God's relation to Him is feminine.

The male priest stands in the person of Christ (*in persona Christi,* in Latin). He is a sacramental sign of Christ the Bridegroom (Mt 9:15; 25:1–12; Jn 3:27–30; Eph 5) before the Church, His bride (CCC 796). It would not make sense for a woman to try to fulfill this role, anymore than it would for a man to try to be a "mother." There is no inequality here, only the God-given difference between men and women. (For more information about the nature of the priesthood, see the *Decree on the Ministry and Life of Priests* of the Second Vatican Council, *Presbyterorum Ordinis,* no. 2.)

Question #139

"Why aren't women more respected in the Church when the greatest of all women gave birth to Jesus?" Clark K., 14

A. Women are held in very high esteem in the Church. In fact, 85 percent of all Church positions are held by women, according to *Catholic Update,* a national newsletter. As Pope John Paul II has taught:

> When women are able fully to share their gifts with the whole community, the very way in which society understands and organizes itself is improved.... The growing presence of women in social, economic, and political life...is thus a very positive development.... This acknowledgment of their public roles however should not detract from their role within the family.... Here their contribution to the welfare and progress of society, even if its

importance is not sufficiently appreciated, is truly incalculable (John Paul II, *Women: Teachers of Peace*).

Holy women have established religious orders, built monasteries, hospitals, and orphanages; and taught tens of millions of our children. Although some members of the Church have made mistakes regarding the role of women in the past, the Church has been far ahead of society in acknowledging their true importance and allowing them to share their gifts with the Church.

Question #140

"Is feminism compatible with the Catholic faith?"
Maria O., 18

A. It depends on what you mean by feminism. If you mean women should have the same basic human rights as men, then certainly Catholic teaching agrees (Gn 1:27; CCC 355). However, if by feminism you mean that there should be no social distinctions between men and women or that women must be ordained to the priesthood, then the answer is "no." This view is typically called "secular" or "radical feminism."

Secular or radical feminists commonly hold views that are actually contrary to true feminine dignity. For example, a woman's ability to conceive and bear children is a wonderful gift from God. Yet many radical feminists view childbearing as a burden or inconvenience. They often support abortion, contraception, and homosexuality, things that actually degrade women.

Question #141

"Are angels male, female, or neither?"
Christina C., 18

A. Angels are neither male nor female. Being pure spirits, they do not possess the bodily traits of gender (Heb 1:13–14; CCC 328, 330). Even so, in Scripture angels appear as males (Gn 19:1-28, for example). The archangel Gabriel is named (Lk 1:11-20, 26-38), as are Michael (Rv 12:7) and Raphael (Tb 5:4).

But remember: Angels are *spiritual* beings. They have no bodies and therefore no wings either! Even so, angels are often depicted in art as winged male or female forms. This is so we can relate to them on a human level and understand something of their powerful intelligence and energy.

Question #142

"Why can't humans become angels, or can we?"
Shannon L., 17

A. Contrary to popular myth, we *do not* become angels when we die. Human beings and angels are completely different species of beings. Comparing them is like comparing a human to a cat or a dog, only the difference is much greater.

Angels are pure spirits. Human beings, on the other hand, are beings of body and spirit (2 Cor 6:16; CCC 327–28). Although our bodies and spirits separate at death, this is an unnatural condition for humans. We will be complete persons again only in the resurrection of the body (1 Cor 15:35–44; Rv 20:12–13; CCC 999).

Angels, however, are completely themselves right now—as pure spirits without bodies.

Question #143

"Can we lose our guardian angels?" Maria O., 18

A. No. Angels are wonderful gifts from God designated to protect and pray for us (Mt 18:10; Ps 91:11–12). They are more faithful and loving than any human being could conceive of being because they are pure spirits committed to the will of God. The will of God is for all to be saved and come to the knowledge of the truth (1 Tm 2:4).

Therefore, God would never withdraw their support. We can resist our guardian angels' efforts and avoid God's grace (Rom 11:22). But they will continually be there for us, in good times and bad.

Question #144

"Is it true that Satan was originally from heaven and fell from grace? If so, how and why did this occur?" Melissa C., 16

Catholic teaching states that at the beginning of time, God created Satan as a good angel. (Indeed, *all* things created by God are good because He Himself is good. Human beings and angels can become *morally* evil through sin, but they remain *essentially* good.) Satan is said to have been the most glorious of created beings, thus his name Lucifer or "light bearer" (Is 14:12–15; CCC 391).

Then Satan and his angels became evil by their own doing (Jn 8:44; Jude 6–7). They chose not to serve

God. They desired to exalt themselves above their created condition and make themselves independent of God.

Since angels are pure spirits and have perfect intellects, they are not affected by psychological and emotional passions as we are. Their choice for or against God was definitive. The fallen angels understood fully what they were doing and could clearly see what the consequences of their choice would be. As the *Catechism* says: "There is no repentance for the angels after their fall, just as there is no repentance for men after death" (CCC 393). The Book of Revelation tells of the battle between St. Michael the Archangel and Satan. Satan and his angels were defeated and cast out of heaven (Lk 10:18; Rv 12:3–9).

Scripture is clear on the subject. Jesus said, "Out of my sight, you condemned, into that everlasting fire prepared for the devil and his angels" (Mt 25:41). God did not spare the angels when they sinned but condemned them to the chains of Tartarus (a name which meant "infernal region" in Greek mythology).

Question #145
"What does the devil look like?" Jimmy C., 14

A. Because he is a spirit, Satan has no physical appearance. The portrayals in Scripture are intended to show his spiritual, not his physical, traits. Thus he is depicted as a malevolent beast (1 Pt 5:8), a beguiling serpent (Gn 3:1), and a dragon (Rv 12:3). In art he is often depicted as a beast with horns or a dark, bat-like figure, sometimes with a goat's head.

Like other angels, Satan can assume an earthly appearance. Sts. John Vianney and Stanislaus said they had seen him in the form of a dog.

But the most dangerous form the devil assumes is that of an angel of light (2 Cor 11:14). He appears to be good but, of course, remains evil. This is why some medieval art shows him has a monk with goat horns. The point is that the devil always proposes an evil act to us as something that is good, like the forbidden fruit in the story of Adam and Eve or the power and glory with which he tried to tempt Jesus.

Images of the devil as a red imp with a pitchfork and tail can be dangerous if they cause us not to take the devil seriously. That, of course, is part of Satan's plan. He is never so successful as when we make light of his existence. As C.S. Lewis noted in his classic *The Screwtape Letters*, the devil's greatest success is to get us to deny that he exists. Why? Because then we will not be on guard against him.

Question #146

"Is the Catholic religion the only religion that has saints?" David A., 15

A. All who have made it to heaven are saints. It follows then that all in heaven are Catholic saints, even if they were originally of another religion. They now understand and accept the truth, which is the Catholic faith.

The Eastern Orthodox faith (which formally broke off from the Catholic Church in the year 1054) also recognizes saints. Protestant faiths and many non-Christian religions have "holy men and women" whom they recognize and honor. These people are not formally recognized as canonized saints by the Catholic Church, even though they may be in heaven (CCC 828).

Question #147

"Why do some Catholics wear scapulars?"
Christina C., 18

A. The scapular is a small piece of cloth that belongs to the Carmelite Order, a religious community. Those who wear the scapular are, to a certain degree, affiliated with that order and share in their prayers and good works. As a result of this affiliation and sharing in the order's special devotion to the Mother of Christ, those who wear the scapular in a spirit of true devotion and love have a special claim to Mary's intercession and protection.

A person who wears the scapular is often invested in it by a formal blessing conferred by a priest. This blessing makes a scapular a *sacramental* (CCC 1670) of the Church. Sacramentals do not "confer the grace of the Holy Spirit in the way that the sacraments do, but by the Church's prayer, they prepare us to receive grace and dispose us to cooperate with it" (CCC 1670). Sacramentals are like little reminders of the sacraments. Holy water is a little reminder of baptism. Blessed oil is a reminder of the sacrament of anointing of the sick. And scapulars can remind us of the sacrament of holy orders since they are tiny versions of the special garments priests wore in the Middle Ages.

On the surface, some people may think scapulars are superstitious "good luck charms" that guarantee our entrance into heaven. They do not. Only being in a state of grace at our death will guarantee our eternal salvation (Rom 11:22). However, scapulars are a special gift from God by which we can attain protective graces.

The Blessed Virgin Mary appeared to St. Simon Stock in the year 1251. She promised that all who wear the brown scapular "shall not suffer eternal fire; and, if wearing it when they die, they shall be saved." This assumes, of course, that one does not deliberately lead a sinful life and make a mockery of God's law.

Question #148

"Why do altars contain relics?" Ed H., 18

A. The Eucharist is the sacrificial offering of Christ to the Father for us. By means of the Holy Spirit, martyrs united themselves and their sacrifices with the sacrifice of Christ on Calvary. Hence, in the early Church it was frequently seen as fitting that the Eucharist be celebrated over their burial sites. The Christians said Mass in the catacombs, the burial places of martyrs. (In fact, that is why St. Peter's Church is where it is, because tradition holds that the bones of St. Peter are buried there.) Offering the Mass at Christian burial sites pointed to the Christian expectation of the resurrection of the body (Rv 20:12–13; 1 Cor 15:51–53).

As time passed, there were more churches than holy sites. So the Church decided to bring the relic to the church instead of the church to the site of the relic. Thus began our practice of placing small pieces of relics in the actual altars in churches.

Chapter 10

CATHOLIC MORALITY

Question #149

"Are Catholics allowed to have an abortion for any reason?" Katie V., 14

A. Since abortion is the direct taking of an innocent human life, one may never deliberately have an abortion or assist another in doing so (Ex 20:13; CCC 2271). I realize there are difficult situations, such as when a pregnancy jeopardizes the mother's life, the child is conceived through rape or incest, or the child is severely handicapped. These hardships should not be minimized. But as difficult (even tragic) as they may be, such circumstances do not justify killing an innocent human being.

Furthermore, thanks to modern medicine, situations in which the life of the mother is truly at risk are extremely rare.

Direct abortion must be distinguished from *indirect abortion.* An indirect abortion occurs when an unborn child's death is an unintentional and indirect consequence of a necessary intervention to treat a dangerous medical condition.

One such condition is the ectopic pregnancy or tubal pregnancy, where the child implants and begins to develop outside the uterus (usually in the fallopian tube). This can pose a serious threat to the mother's life. Under the moral principle of *double effect,* diseased or dangerous tissue of the fallopian tube can be removed, even if the tissue is also the location of the implanted fetus. The death of the fetus is an unfortunate and *unintended* (although foreseen) consequence of removing the diseased tissue.

Although certain principles can be stated regarding situations such as ectopic pregnancies, the moral evaluation of medical procedures in specific cases can differ. Consultation with a sound Catholic moral theologian and a medical doctor would be advised in this type of case.

Regarding rape or incest, research suggests that the woman carrying the baby will much sooner forget the rape or incest than the abortion (see the book *Victims and Victors* for a more detailed discussion of this point [Acorn Books, 2000]). Human beings know deep down that abortion is wrong. This is why so many women suffer depression and other psychological problems after abortions.

Regarding handicapped children, it is very dangerous when individuals are allowed to decide whether someone else should live simply because that person is perceived to be of less value due to a physical ailment (CCC 274). A person's value is not determined by what he or she does or is like (Mt 5:3, 5). People with disabilities have much to offer society. And even if a person is severely disabled and unable to function on his or her own, that person is still a gift from God who can bring tremendous love to a family and society. They are to be embraced and viewed with the respect and value they deserve.

We should also be reminded that our Lord wants all involved with the sin of abortion to seek forgiveness. He welcomes with open arms those who have had abortions if they turn back to Him (Ez 18:23, 30).

Question #150

"I know abortion is wrong, but how can I tell others why it is wrong?" Caitlin H., 15

A. There are two approaches you can take. The first is to use moral principles that all people generally accept. The second is to appeal to revelation.

Begin with the idea that no one has the right to take the life of an innocent person. Then discuss how the baby is a separate human being, distinct from his or her mother. Each child has his or her own unique genetic identity, gender, heartbeat, brain waves, eyes, hands, feet, and so on. Challenge others to consider whether society is actually moving backward or forward when it permits its young to be killed as a solution to its problems. Acknowledge that women do have certain rights over their bodies, just as men do, but these rights are limited when they affect other people's rights. Abortion directly involves at least two bodies: the body of the mother and that of her unborn child. The child's rights are being radically denied in abortion.

Then discuss what has been revealed by God. Point out that the Bible teaches that children are a gift from God.

God knows each child from his or her first moment in the womb (Jer 1:5; Is 41:2, 44:24; CCC 2270). Then ask the person, "Do you think God is pleased that His precious gifts are being brutally killed in what should be the safest place on earth—the mother's womb?"

If people tell you not to bring religion into the discussion, point out that everything is ultimately a religious issue. God's laws exist. They are not made up by man. You are simply sharing what these laws are (Ex 20:13). Their argument then is really with God, not with the pro-life movement.

Question #151

"Are you allowed to use birth control if you are a Catholic?" Kay B., 15

A. Your question is very important, but complicated, so I will have to spend some time addressing it.

Does the Church allow birth control? It depends on what you mean by "birth control." Birth control, as the name suggests, regulates the birth of children. Consequently, birth control can include things such as contraception and abortion as well as Natural Family Planning (NFP).

Contraception is "any action which, either in anticipation of the conjugal act, or in its accomplishment, or in the development of its natural consequences, proposes, whether as an end or as a means, to render procreation impossible" (*Humanae Vitae*, no. 14; CCC 2370). Abortion is the deliberate and direct ending of a pregnancy, terminating the life of an innocent, unborn child. Both contaception and abortion are morally unacceptable means of "regulating birth" or "birth control," although abortion (and the forms of artificial contraception that can actually cause abortions) is the graver of the two immoral acts.

The sin of contraception may be committed by use of contraceptive pills, condoms, spermicides, physical or chemical "barriers," sterilization, and other means. None of these are morally acceptable forms of family planning.

On the other hand, there are morally acceptable means of "regulating births." NFP uses the signs of a woman's natural monthly cycle to determine fertility. If the couple wants to avoid conceiving a child, they can abstain from sexual intercourse during this fertile period.

One of the most awesome gifts God gave us is the ability to generate new life made in His image. Human beings are co-creators with God in this process. Contraception deliberately thwarts this God-given gift by treating conception as an evil to be avoided.

God designed sexual intercourse with two inherent meanings. These meanings are "written into" the act itself. They are the "unitive" or person-uniting meaning (Gn 2:24) and the "procreative" or person-begetting meaning (Gn 1:28). These two meanings are interrelated and are intended by God to be present in every act of intercourse (CCC 1643, 2366).

Every act of intercourse need not result in procreation. God designed things in such a way that this does not always happen. But each act of intercourse should have, by its nature or the kind of act it is, the possibility of new life and the reality of enacting loving union between the husband and wife. The act should have a procreative meaning even if, here and now, procreation does not occur.

Contraception, as I have said, deprives sexual intercourse of its procreative meaning. It turns it into an act that is actually hostile to new life. How so? By taking something like the pill, wearing something like a condom, or otherwise doing something directly and intentionally opposed to new life.

Consider an analogy: Let's say I want to lose weight. One way is to avoid foods that have a lot of calories. But what if I ate a large piece of chocolate cake, savored the taste, swallowed it, but then, to avoid gaining weight, I made myself vomit? I enjoyed the goodness of the cake, but then used the unnatural act of forced vomiting to avoid the consequences.

The natural purpose of eating is to nourish the body. Eating is intended to be a pleasurable act, but the pleasure that accompanies the act should not be our only purpose for eating. We should not eat in such a way that we actually thwart the nourishing purpose of eating. People who do that have an eating disorder.

Contraception is similar. People contracept to avoid a natural consequence of the sex act—conception—but still have the pleasure. In doing so they attack one of the basic goods (new life) inherent in the act. And not only do they hurt the procreative meaning of intercourse, they also attack its unitive or person-uniting meaning. People who contracept withhold a very important part of themselves in their lovemaking: their power to generate with another a being *made in God's image*. They do not really give their whole selves to their spouse in intercourse; they do not fully become "one flesh" in that sense.

We live in an age when children are often viewed with contempt. They are seen as burdens, liabilities, and obstacles to personal freedom. This is an anti-life mentality that too often manifests itself in families in which the parents are more concerned with material gain and leisure than with raising children for God. Sure, children are challenging to raise, but ultimately they bring far greater joy and love to the family than do worldly pursuits.

Question #152

"Although Natural Family Planning isn't artificial like condoms and birth control pills, isn't birth control by its very nature unnatural?"
Ernesto O., 17

A. Properly used, Natural Family Planning is not unnatural. Before we can see why, though, I should explain how NFP works.

Modern studies of human reproduction have shown that most women's ova are viable only twelve to twenty-four hours. This means that pregnancy can only occur one to eight days a month, according to most fertility experts. NFP uses natural indicators in a woman's body (such as the presence and texture of cervical mucus, changes in body temperature, and so on) to determine when she is fertile and the likelihood that conception could occur (CCC 2370). That means NFP can be used either to avoid conception or to increase the chances of conception by identifying when a women has ovulated.

Is there anything unnatural or morally wrong with a couple wanting to avoid pregnancy? Not necessarily. Although one of the essential purposes of marriage is the procreation of children, there may be physical, social, and even psychological circumstances in which a couple is prudent to avoid conceiving a child. Obviously, such circumstances should be serious, not frivolous.

NFP *can* be abused, as when a couple avoids having a child for purely selfish reasons. However, in itself, NFP merely allows a couple to avoid intercourse during times when conception is most likely to occur. It is *non*-conceptive, not *contra*ceptive. It cooperates with nature, with the natural cycle of a woman's body, to determine when sexual intercourse will be non-conceptive; it does not alter the act of intercourse to make it anti-conceptive.

Abstaining from sexual relations for good reasons is not unnatural. There might be all sorts of reasons for spouses to abstain—health, family concerns, timing, to name a few. Human beings have minds, which God expects us to use. There is nothing wrong with using good judgment about when to have children and when to avoid doing so (CCC 2368) However, if despite our plans children come anyway, we must accept them as persons to be valued, rather than as burdens to be avoided.

NFP respects our human nature; it does not alter or attack it as contraception does. NFP is not "natural" contraception. Contraception involves positively acting to alter the procreative nature of intercourse (CCC 2370). It takes an act that would otherwise be procreative (open to new life) and closes it by means of drugs, physical barriers, or actions. Contraception *opposes* a natural outcome of intercourse: conception.

Question #153

"If you could not have children, would it be OK to use artificial insemination instead of adopting children?" Christine J., 16

A. Be sure to read my answer to the end, because this is another one of those difficult questions that require an openness to the Church's explanations of and its authority on questions of morality.

No, artificial insemination is not morally acceptable. Children should be "begotten, not made." Although parents who engage in artificial insemination may be well-intentioned, the means they choose to bring new life into existence is morally unacceptable (CCC 2376). It amounts to manufacturing people by a technological process, rather than allowing human beings to be begotten by a truly human act of self-donating love (sexual intercourse) (CCC 2377).

Further, artificial insemination treats children as a "right" to be "owned" rather than a gift to be received. Children are not our "property"; they are persons whom God entrusts to us. If, in his Providence, we are not entrusted with children, we cannot override God's will and claim our "rights" against Him.

Remember, for an act to be morally acceptable, the *means* (the way one does something) as well as the *end* (what a person wishes to achieve) must be morally good.

There is no doubt that a couple's inability to have children can be extremely painful and frustrating. But this does not make it acceptable to have a child through artificial insemination, any more than it would make it acceptable to kidnap someone else's child because he or she already has ten children. The end does not justify the means.

What about fertility drugs to help couples have children? The idea of using a drug to help fertility is not, in itself, a moral problem. But there are some related issues that can be, so the matter needs to be carefully thought through and all the health risks considered, both to the mother and her potential offspring (CCC 2375, 2377).

For example, sometimes fertility drugs result in the conception of multiple children—not just twins or triplets, but even septuplets. To diminish health risks to the mother or to some children in the womb, doctors may propose "selective terminations"—abortions, in other words—of some of the embryonic babies. That is not morally acceptable; it amounts to unjustly killing innocent human beings.

Imagine how you would feel knowing that your brother or sister was "selectively terminated." You could just as easily have been the baby terminated before birth.

Although infertility may be difficult to accept, God may allow it for certain couples in order to challenge them to open their hearts to adoption (CCC 2379). There are countless children here and abroad in need of loving parents. Adoption is a better, more loving, and safer choice than artificial insemination—and a moral one.

Question #154

"Is dating OK?" Danny N., 14

A. Of course, if done with respect for God's laws and for the person you are dating. Healthy dating can lead to healthy and stable marriages.

Although chaste dating for the mere fun of companionship is acceptable, it is important to remember that finding a marriage partner is the primary goal of dating. This is why it is so important to be prudent in our dating choices and perspectives. Healthy marriages are the foundation of a healthy and stable society (CCC 1603).

Society's influence (especially that of television) forces people to think they are weird or incomplete if they are not in a "hot and heavy" dating relationship. This is a lie. The emotional charge that dating gives is not its primary purpose.

Although dating offers a chance to develop interpersonal skills, which will be helpful in married life or religious life, there are other ways to do this. You do not have to worry you are weird if you do not date a lot (or at all). Do not let yourself be forced into dating someone you do not want to date or *before* you truly want to.

Question #155

"How old do you have to be to date if you're a Catholic?" Kay B., 15

A. There is no specific age, but in my opinion, a Catholic who is serious about his or her faith should probably wait *at least* until the late high school years before casually dating. Some would even say a person should wait until well into their college years. There are many things to accomplish and focus on in your high school and college years other than dating. Let yourself mature so that you can make good dating choices. Develop your talents and abilities; this is good for you personally and will make you more aware of the qualities you want in someone you date. Most importantly, get to know God better and seek His will for your life (Prv 3:5-6; Ps 39).

Question #156

"Is there hope for a young Catholic to find a good Catholic spouse in this society?" Ed H., 18

A. You sound like a young man who is trying to live a virtuous life.

Yes, there are surely tens of thousands of young ladies who are also trying to live virtuous lives. In fact, a recent *Newsweek* cover story entitled "The New Virginity" (December 9, 2002) noted a new trend among teens towards chastity and virtuous living.

My advice is to stay strong, have faith, and pray a novena to St. Raphael, who is a patron saint of finding that special someone (read the Book of Tobit for his story). Spend time in places where you can meet a committed Catholic young person, such as church, a young adult group, a college Newman center, or even a respected Catholic dating service. You should also pray for discernment about what your true vocation is. You may be destined to marry the most wonderful bride of all, the Church, in a religious vocation.

Question #157

"Is it OK to date a non-Catholic?" Nicollete C., 16

A. It is certainly possible to find "Mr. or Miss Right" in another faith. However, a mutual outlook on life, which clearly comes from a shared Catholic faith, is vital to a successful dating relationship and marriage.

The primary goal of dating is to find a suitable marriage partner. Good marriages most often come from healthy dating relationships. We should not date merely to satisfy some emotional or physical need.

While a successful marriage between a Catholic and non-Catholic Christian (or even a non-Christian) is possible, such marriages bring with them special challenges (CCC 1633–34). Marriage requires hard work. It will be even harder if there are religious differences.

Scripture speaks of binding yourself to someone who is on the same spiritual level as you. "Do not be yoked with those who are different, with an unbeliever. For what partnership do righteousness and lawlessness have" (2 Cor 6:14)? This is why the Church generally encourages Catholics to marry other Catholics.

Question #158

"Why is my dad so strictly against my going out with non-Catholic boys?" Patti H., 16

A. Your father knows that casual dating often leads to serious dating. And serious dating is part of the process by which we find our future spouses.

No doubt your dad would prefer that you marry a Catholic boy. He believes in the Catholic faith and would like his daughter to marry someone who does, too. He knows that a couple who share the same faith will be better prepared to handle the challenges all marriages face. So he is really looking out for your happiness.

Question #159

"In a relationship, how far is 'too far' before it is considered a sin?" Jolene N., 17

A. We are made in the image and likeness of God, which means we cannot treat another person as an object of pleasure (Gn 1:26). Therefore, actions that directly stimulate sexual passion (like touching another's sexual organs) are morally unacceptable (1 Tm 5:22). Our sexual gifts have a much higher and special purpose.

Actions like holding hands, modest kisses, and embraces are perfectly fine as long as you have a firm presence of mind that these acts will not lead to serious sins against chastity. Sins against chastity are sins against the sixth and ninth commandments (Ex 20:14, 17).

Loose sexual behavior becomes a tyrant that keeps making more demands on those involved. Eventually, you and your date will get bored with just kissing and will most likely want to move on to other things. This is called the "law of diminishing returns." Kissing does not always give the same excitement as when you first did it. The more one feeds these passions, the more one's will becomes weakened.

Also, because guys tend to be more physically oriented than girls, they often stop doing the healthy and morally acceptable things that they used to do with their dates before sex entered the relationship. Activities like going to the mall or movies seem to go by the wayside once the two become sexually active. Girls who give in to the sexual demands of guys in order to "strengthen the relationship" often find that guys lose interest in the relationship and just want to go straight to sex. Guys who form these habits are not preparing for a life of self-giving love but a lifetime of self-centeredness.

Even when a man and woman are engaged to be married, they must live chastely. The covenant and consecrated relationship begins only when they confer upon one another the sacrament of marriage with the blessing of God and the Church. The couple must reserve for marriage any expression of affection that belongs to married love.

Question #160

"Is French kissing OK?" Josh M., 13

A. Although it is exciting, passionate kissing or embracing can be a near occasion of sin and is probably venially sinful. In and of itself it is not a mortal sin, but it can easily lead to greater sin because it naturally stimulates desire for more intimate contact. Two unmarried people should avoid getting "hot and heavy" with deep kissing, because this almost always leads to more serious actions (1 Thess 4:3–8).

Here is an analogy: Let's say you were driving down a steep hill in a three-ton truck with a six-hundred-pound piano on the back. Would you first put on the brakes ten feet before the intersection? Certainly not. You would put on the brakes at the top of the hill and ease the truck and piano down the hill. The same prudence should guide dating relationships. Take them slow.

A modest kiss or embrace is perfectly fine, but beware of getting too physically intimate. It will only make things harder in the end and may take you down a road you really do not want to travel at this point in your life.

Today's teens should not be preoccupied with dating as much as they are. They should focus on schooling, extracurricular activities like sports or drama, and developing skills for a future career. I know chaste dating can be difficult at times, but you can do it if you practice virtue and seek God's grace (Phil 4:13; 2 Cor 12:8–9; CCC 2340).

Question #161

"Why is there so much sex going on with teens today as compared to when my parents were young?" Daniel N., 17

A. I am guessing, based on your age, that your parents spent their teenage years in the late 1960s or 1970s. And quite frankly, those were the years that started much of the mess we have today. Unfortunately, things have gotten worse.

The number one reason why teens are having more premarital sex today is because Satan is working overtime (1 Pt 5:8). It is important to remember that any sinful act is ultimately prompted by the workings of Satan, who desires that we lose our soul (Rom 7:15–25).

The second biggest reason is the invention of artificial birth control. Those who grew up before birth control was widespread had the same sexual urges, but they had a tremendous fear of unwed pregnancy because of the bad reputation that went along with it. Contraception misleads people into thinking they need not fear unwanted pregnancy or sexually transmitted disease. Therefore, contraception actually *encourages* premarital sex.

A third factor is the decline in morals throughout society. Much of society, especially the media, has little concern for modesty. A 2001 study by the Kaiser Family Foundation noted that 3 out of 4 prime time TV shows contain sexual references (most often to sexual activity outside of marriage), and 84 percent of sitcoms contain sexual references. Most would agree that television has gotten worse in recent years.

Also, the bad consequences of premarital sex are almost never portrayed on television. The stars of the popular TV shows never seem to have broken hearts, get pregnant, suffer hemorrhages from abortions, or suffer the horrible effects of a sexually transmitted disease. They seem to have wonderful lives. This, of course, is not reality. Thousands of these tragedies occur *every day* to people as a result of premarital sex.

There are many other reasons why more teens are having sex today than in years past, including earlier dating, more broken homes (which cause loneliness and a greater search for intimacy) and increasing peer pressure. If you're interested in more on this topic, refer to the books *If You Love Me* by Jason Evert, *Why Wait?* by Josh McDowell and Dick Day, and *Real Love* by Mary Beth Bonacci. They are listed in the Resources section.

Question #162

"Is sex before marriage a sin?" John H., 14

A. This is an important answer, so I ask that you take your time to read it completely.

Yes, premarital sex is a sin (Gal 5:19–21; 1 Cor 6:9–10; Eph 5:5; CCC 2353). Unfortunately, too many young people have not been taught the reasons why sex before marriage is wrong, so many of them have fallen into this lifestyle. Today's teens may be judged by an easier standard because of their ignorance, but there is no guarantee that this will be the case.

I believe that if you have clear answers about *why* God says we are to remain chaste, you will be better equipped to save the precious gift of your sexuality for its proper use and time (CCC 2343).

As you know, God invented sex. And because God invented sex, we know that it is a good thing (Gn 1:31)! Anything that God makes or institutes is good, because He is good. However, with any good thing comes certain responsibilities. Why? Because God does not want the good thing to become a source of pain, evil, selfishness, or death. He wants sex to be the absolutely profound and wonderful act it was meant to be. He gave us the sexual attraction to bring the two sexes together in a way that would lead to marriage and procreation, which is the *ultimate* (not the only, but the ultimate) purpose of marriage (Gn 1:28; CCC 2366).

Think about it. God can do anything He wants. He could have brought new humans into the world by another means. He might have established a world in which He was the *sole* creator of the human person, body and soul, without human interaction. The male/female relationship could have been just a platonic friendship. He could have created us to reproduce asexually, like bacteria. But no, God established a system of reproduction that included humans. He chose the sexual act as the means by which the creation of humans, whom He would endow with an invaluable soul, would be achieved (CCC 2367).

The soul of a new baby will last for all eternity. Because the human person, especially the soul, is so valuable and important, the sexual act *must* be important. And like most important things, it is logical to think sex has a proper and an improper use.

Besides the tremendous pain, selfishness, and evil that can come with sex outside of marriage (including broken hearts, abortion, diseases, hardened hearts, and low self-esteem), premarital sex can easily lead to unwed pregnancies. Unwed pregnancies involve all sorts of problems, especially for women. A 1998 Ohio State University study showed that unwed pregnancies lead to a cycle of poverty, illiteracy, abuse, maladjusted children, emotional disturbances (like a desperate search for intimacy). While there may be exceptions to this, they are few.

We humans speak with more than words. We speak with our bodies as well. When two people bare their bodies to each other, they also bare their souls. They basically say to each other, "I am exclusively yours and you are exclusively mine... And I will never leave you or hurt you." Yet, with premarital sex this rarely ends up being the case. Too many relationships end up with heartache, pain, a physical side effect, and even a loss of religious faith. With premarital sex, one has almost everything to lose and very little to gain. The two people tell each other lies with their bodies, promising their all, but withholding themselves from full commitment.

The sexual act between two people is the most intimate expression of human love possible. It really only makes sense within a committed lifelong relationship— marriage (CCC 2337, 2361).

Question #163

"If you plan to marry someone, is it OK to have sex before the wedding?" Shelley T., 14

A. Before I answer your question, let me show you two actual letters people wrote to columnist Ann Landers that I found in the book *Why Wait?* (which I mentioned earlier). They say a lot.

The first was written by a woman:

I met him; I liked him.

I liked him; I loved him

I loved him; I let him

I let him; I lost him.

The second was written by a man:

I saw her.

I liked her.

I loved her.

I wanted her.

I asked her.

She said no.

I married her.

After sixty years,

I still have her.

No good intention ever justifies doing an evil act. For example, we could not sell drugs to raise money for the poor, because we know that evil will result from selling drugs. Doing an evil act is like shooting a gun blindly into a crowd; it is likely that a bullet will hit someone. Likewise, we know that problems will result from having sex outside of marriage even if the goal is to express sincere love.

The Bible is very clear on the spiritual fate of those who sin against God (and their own bodies) through premarital sex *and who do not repent before they die.* St. Paul says, "Do not be deceived; neither fornicators, nor idolaters, nor adulterers, nor boy prostitutes, nor practicing homosexuals ... will inherit the kingdom of God" (1 Cor 6:9–10; Gal 5:19–21; Eph 5:5).

We also read: "Avoid [sexual] immorality. Every other sin a person commits is outside the body, but the immoral person sins against his own body. Do you not know that your body is the temple of the Holy Spirit within you, whom you have from God? For you have been purchased at a price. Therefore, glorify God in your body" (1 Cor 6:18–20).

Jesus' death on the cross opened up the gates of heaven and gave us the hope of eternal life. He purchased us at a great price. It is a serious offense to our Savior to disregard His commandments and make up our own religious and moral beliefs.

While you may believe that you will be with your boyfriend all your life, there are no guarantees. An overwhelming percentage of teenage relationships break up after short periods of time. And for people of all ages, premarital sex is unhealthy for relationships. A recent University of Wisconsin study showed that couples who lived together before marriage had a 50 percent higher divorce rate than those who did not. Couples who had abstained from sex before marriage were up to 47 percent more satisfied with their marital relationships than those who had slept together before marriage.

When sex is introduced into a dating relationship, things start to change almost immediately. The two people, especially the girl, often become anxious and preoccupied with worries about the relationship. The relationship occupies too much of their time and affects their schooling, friends, family relationships, self-esteem, and most importantly, their relationship with God.

Question #164

"If you love the person, I don't think it should matter if you have sex before you are married."
Jeanette C., 15

A. True love involves sacrifice. It also involves *fidelity*, which means faithfulness. Think about it. If you and your boyfriend are not faithful to God's laws, what evidence is there that you will be faithful to each other?

I would tell the girls in my former youth group: "If a guy will not sacrifice for you and is willing to subject you to the many problems that come with premarital sex, then he doesn't *really* love you. He may be infatuated with you. He may have fun with you. But he doesn't *truly* love you. True love is much different."

The definition of love is "to want what is best for the other simply because it is best for that person" (and not because you will get something out of it). Can a boy *really* say he loves a girl if he is willing to subject her to physical danger (unmarried pregnancy, the side effects of birth control, and sexually transmitted diseases) and the emotional stress (heartache, anxiety) of a sexual relationship?

And what about the spiritual dangers? Can you imagine a boyfriend saying, "I love you, so let's risk going to hell together"? I do not think someone who *really* loves you would subject you to this risk.

Love is based on friendship (CCC 2347), and a friendship is really not a good one if it leads to sin, troubles one's conscience, lowers one's ideals, and weakens one's faith (Sir 6:7–17).

If two people really love each other, they will want the relationship to last. I challenge young teens who are dating to treat the other person like a brother or sister in Christ—because that is who the person is. He or she is *literally* God's adopted son or daughter—as you are (CCC 2782). This makes you a spiritual brother or sister to the person. Would you do something evil to one of God's children (Mt 18:6, 10)?

Unmarried couples should show modest affection toward each other. If a couple is already sexually active, they should stop the sexual activity *and remain chaste until marriage* (1 Tm 5:22; Rom 12:1; CCC 2348–50). If they do, they stand a much better chance of staying together and avoiding marriage problems later on.

Question #165

"Besides catching a disease or getting a girl pregnant, what are the other negative affects of having premarital sex? My girlfriend and I love each other and feel we are ready." Peter C., 17

A. Sexual activity is such an important and powerful act because it is the means by which God brings new souls into the world. Used properly, it is a gift from God that can bring about great joy and union between two married people. Used improperly, it can bring great pain and hardship, especially for teenagers who are, generally speaking, less prepared to handle the emotional, social, and spiritual consequences of illicit sex.

If "diseases" and "getting a girl pregnant" are not enough reasons to abstain from sex, I am not sure I will be able to satisfy you at all. Nevertheless, here are fifteen other reasons to save sex for marriage:

1. *Premarital sex inhibits your ability to love truly.* Although physical intimacy can bring two people closer together, it can also be the very thing that stifles love and communication, especially for men. Men tend to focus very much on the physical pleasure of the relationship. They need to learn how to love and communicate in a relationship. Yet often a guy stops communicating, bringing flowers, and talking sweetly once he becomes sexually active with a girl.

2. *It makes people selfish.* Because teenage pregnancy (and the difficulties that come with it) may result, premarital sex is a very selfish thing for two people to do. They are putting a baby's future in jeopardy because of the problems that most young married and unmarried teen parents face. These problems include low-paying jobs, a greater dependence on welfare, and less experience in preparing children to face the countless challenges presented by the world. It is selfish to think of one's own pleasure and disregard the possibility of really hurting others, especially children that could result from the sex act.

3. *It preoccupies your mind.* Young people should be worrying about the next math test, not the next pregnancy test. I have seen young girls and guys get all their energy "zapped" out of them after they became sexually active. Why? Because premarital sex can be "all consuming." It tends to occupy one's thoughts. Girls become more anxious, with thoughts of guilt and low self-worth and guys get consumed with the thought of repeating the act.

4. *It leads to broken hearts.* Think about how many guys and girls have had broken hearts after a breakup, especially when they see their "ex" with another person. Sex creates a bond between people. When the bond is broken, hearts can be torn in two. Scientists may have invented a condom that can prevent pregnancy, but no scientist will ever invent a condom to protect against a broken heart.

5. *It causes guilt.* Premarital sex is sort of like stealing. You know you are taking what really isn't yours. Unconfessed sin and the guilt that comes with premarital sex cause all kinds of problems, including the hardening of one's heart and mild neuroses, including anxiety. Living a chaste life liberates you (1 Pt 2:11; Mt 5:8, CCC 2339). When we live the truth, we are truly set free (Jn 8:31-32).

6. *Premarital sex can make you marry the wrong person.* Sex is powerful. It creates a bond between two people. A sexually-active relationship can cause spiritual and emotional blindness in one or both parties. You may "fall in love" with a person who is bad for you.

7. *Premarital sex is really a lie to the other person.* Sexual intimacy is much more than a physical act. There really is much more going on in the hearts, minds, and souls of the two persons than you might think. Sex speaks a "language"—a language of love, faithfulness, and commitment. Two people say with their bodies, "I give my whole self to you." But in reality they have not done that or they would be married. Even if a couple is engaged, they have not really promised

themselves wholly and exclusively to one another. They have only *promised* to promise. Before marriage, sex between two people is a form of deceit, for they really would not (and could not) mean what they say by their actions.

8. *It causes future jealousies.* Both men and women can suffer flashbacks or jealous pangs at the thought of their spouse or "significant other" being intimate with someone else.

9. *It may lead to sexual dissatisfaction once one is married.* When a person gets married to someone after being sexually active with others, there is a greater chance of dissatisfaction with the marital love life because of comparisons with past experiences. A person who has not engaged in sexual activity will appreciate his or her spouse and their love life much more.

10. *You only have one "first time."* Wouldn't sex be much nicer if you were to wait until your honeymoon? After being chaste with your wife during your courtship, the reward is much greater.

11. *It causes awkwardness and tension.* Nervously fornicating in the back seat of the car or in your parents' basement does not compare to the true peace of marital sex. In marriage, you know that you and your spouse have a clear conscience because God has blessed your union.

12. *It may lead to sexual addictions or problems.* Sex is a powerful act. Most people cannot psychologically or emotionally handle premarital

sex. Why? Because sex is more than just a physical act, especially for girls. When a person gives his or her body to another, this person is also giving a piece of his or her soul to the other. Treating the body as a mere toy or object of gratification creates a real distortion in the minds of the user and the used. As a result, sexual addictions and perversions can develop.

13. *It can lead to a lack of trust of the opposite sex.* A relationship that "goes sour" can stay with someone and can affect that person's next relationship. People who have felt "used" by others have a problem trusting. This can lead to divorce, which can bring about a whole host of problems, especially for children of the marriage.

14. *You are jeopardizing your salvation.* God is very clear on the topic. Sex is His gift for the married couple. God said it, so that should settle it. Unfortunately, the world is pushing God's teachings out of society. People, especially the young, are not being taught these profound truths. Subsequently, many will risk losing their souls by living unchaste lives and not repenting before death (Eph 5:5; Gal 5:19–21; 1 Cor 6:9–10).

15. *It may lead another astray.* Let's say you repent and are eventually saved. What if the girl or boy you introduced sex to in high school never turns back? You may be partly the cause of that person's path of spiritual destruction (Mt 18:6–7)? Are you ready to stand before Jesus with that on your conscience?

I think that if you seriously consider and pray about these fifteen truths, you will see the logic in following God's call to chastity.

Question #166

"There is a lot of sexual temptation out there. How can a person survive until marriage?" Dennis S., 18

A. Here are ten ways you can have healthy dating relationships and remain chaste. Several of them are from the books, *Why Wait?* and *Real Love*, which I mentioned earlier and which are listed in the Resources section.

1. *Pray.* Talk to Jesus (Phil 4:13; 2 Cor 12:9). Also ask for the prayers of the saints, especially St. Maria Goretti, who is the patron saint of chastity.

2. *Say three "Hail Mary's" every day for purity.* If you ask, Our Lady will pray that God will give you the grace to stay pure.

3. *Frequent the sacraments (especially reconciliation).* Jesus gives us supernatural help in the seven sacraments in a powerful way (Jn 6:56; CCC 1084, 2345).

4. *Know that you are not alone.* There are many other teens who also believe that being chaste is a better way to live. (For more information on this point, see the December, 9, 2002 issue of *Newsweek* magazine for wonderful stories about teens embracing chastity by vowing to wait for sex until they are married.)

5.   *Set high standards.* The person who stands for nothing falls for everything. So set high standards.

6.   *Have the courage to leave bad relationships.* Do not stay in a relationship that is causing you to sin (Mt 5:29–30).

7.   *Value the other person.* Remember that the guy or girl you are thinking of being sexually active with could be someone else's future husband or wife. Would you want someone fooling around with your future spouse? If not, then you should not be fooling around with someone else's future spouse (Ex 20:14; Mt 5:27–28).

8.   *Have someone to talk to.* If your parents are not available, speak to a priest, sibling, or youth minister with whom you feel comfortable and who is supportive of Church teaching.

9.   *Date responsibly.* Set goals, time limits, and specific dating plans. Also consider dating in groups, with at least one other couple, so you do not get into a dangerous situation.

10.   *Pray with your date.* Wouldn't that be cool? At the very least, say a private prayer before the date.

If you have already engaged in premarital sex, you can become a "second-time virgin" or a "virgin in your head." You will not get your physical virginity back, but you *can* make a commitment from this day forth to wait until you are married. Would you never save money again if you spent all that was in your savings account?

Of course not. The same applies to premarital sex. If you made a mistake, repent and vow not to make the same mistake again.

Question #167

"Is masturbation a sin? If so, why?"
Name and age withheld

A. Yes, masturbation is a sin. Our sexual organs are not playthings to be used for self-gratification (CCC 2352). They are intended for sexual relations in marriage, to express and share mutual, self-donating love, and for the procreation of children.

When we use our sexual power of loving and procreating within marriage according to God's purpose, we honor Him and our bodies. When we do not, we dishonor God and our bodies, something Scripture condemns (Rom 1:24).

Masturbation is often called "self-abuse" precisely because the person who masturbates abuses his or her body, which is a temple of the Holy Spirit (Rom. 12:1; CCC 364). Masturbation is a sin against nature—which was designed and given order by God (Gn 38:9–10). In masturbation, it is pleasure alone that becomes the end goal, not the joy found in doing something truly loving.

Masturbation is also very dangerous to one's social and interpersonal skills, because it is a selfish act that turns the person inward. It makes one self-absorbed. Masturbation can also make someone a selfish spouse who is only concerned about his or her own sexual pleasure. This, of course, could be harmful to marriage.

There are many faithful priests who will say that, although the act is objectively sinful, the subjective (that is, personal) guilt of someone today *may* not be present due to immaturity, the widespread sexual messages in the media, and the lack of proper catechetical formation of today's youth. *This should not, however, give someone license to sin.* Masturbation is sinful, and its negative effects still exist regardless of a person's subjective guilt. For anyone who has a problem with this sin, I recommend the person find a good priest with whom he or she feels comfortable. Ask him for spiritual direction and prayer.

Question #168

"Is pornography wrong?" Clark K., 14

A. Yes, it is sinful for a number of reasons (CCC 2354). The first reason is because it fosters impure thoughts, which are sins against the sixth and ninth commandments (Ex 20:14,17). Second, it easily leads to impure actions such as masturbation, fornication, and adultery. Third, it can bring about a desire for unnatural sex acts because pornography presents a warped view of human sexuality (2 Pt 2:9–17; CCC 2352–53, 2380).

According to a study done at the University of Utah, pornography:

1. stimulates and arouses aggressive sexual feelings;
2. shows and instructs in detail how to do the act;
3. legitimizes the act through repeated exposure, and increases the likelihood the viewer will act out what he or she sees.

Another study at New York University showed that

repeated viewing of pornography leads to an increase in rape. In interviews given before their deaths, serial killers Ted Bundy and Jeffrey Dahmer stated that their addiction to pornography contributed to their dehumanization of their victims, which made killing them much easier. Some experts have said that pornography can be as addictive as some of the most potent drugs.

Pornography deadens the senses. It reduces the opposite sex to a mere object of pleasure. It also stifles one's ability to communicate, which will be very harmful to a future dating relationship and to marriage.

Question #169

"What should you do if you try 'second-time virginity' as chastity speakers have suggested, but you end up being sexually active again?" Clare H., 14

A. Go to confession to be reconciled with God, and then try harder (Jas 5:16; Lk 11:4; CCC 1422).

The "second-time virginity" plan should not be viewed as a license to sin again and again. You should *really* do your best to avoid this serious sin (CCC 1431). It is a grave offense against the sixth and ninth commandments (Ex 20:14, 17). If you do fall, get up quickly and reconcile yourself to God, the Church, and if possible, the person with whom you sinned.

You should examine your conscience to see if you really are trying to avoid the near occasions of sin (1 Jn 3:19–20). If not, be more diligent. Also speak with a priest, youth minister, or Christian counselor about the situation (1

Thess 5:12–13). He or she should be able to offer advice on how you can strengthen your walk with the Lord.

Question #170

"Is virginity on the rise or are all teenagers 'doing it'?" Ed H., 18

A. Among religious teens, there is definitely a trend toward chastity. I have already mentioned the *Newsweek* cover story (December 9, 2002) about teens vowing abstinence from sex until marriage. Many new movements in Catholic, Protestant, and other religious circles have started in recent years.

Young people are seeing that it is truly cool and even heroic to live a chaste life (Rom 6:12; Mt 5:8; 1 Thess 4:3–8). They like being different. (It is unfortunate that nowadays a person is considered "different" if he or she is chaste.) Young people are seeing the real peace of mind and heart that comes from living a faithful Christian life (Gal 5:22; Jn 14:27, 16:33).

Regarding teens as a whole, I would say that things are probably getting worse. Without God, things will always get worse (Rom 1:20–25). There are many teens who abstain from sex because of the fear of sexually-transmitted diseases, but many of them will eventually believe the "safe sex" lie and become sexually active.

St. Paul tells us in his letter to the Romans to "transform" ourselves through "the renewal of [our] minds" so that we might "discern what is the will of God, what is good and pleasing and perfect" (Rom 12:2). You can fortify yourself by spending time with friends who have chosen to live chastely and by reading good books on the topic like *If You Love Me* by Jason Evert, *Real Love* by Mary Beth Bonacci, and *Why Wait?* by Josh McDowell and Dick Day. (These are listed in the Resources section at the end of this book.)

So, do not give up. Even if you are the only one left (which you will never be), you will still be right. You will be the one who ultimately has peace of mind and conscience (CCC 2339).

Question #171

"Why is being 'gay' a sin?" Philip T., 15

A. There is a difference between a homosexual *orientation* (that is, finding members of the same gender sexually attractive) and homosexual *acts* (sexual activity between members of the same sex). The Church teaches that homosexual *orientation* is not sinful—though it is an inclination or a tendency toward sinful behavior that must be resisted. Homosexual *acts*, however, are always sinful, because sexual acts are intended by God for husbands and wives, not unmarried persons, whether of the same or opposite sex.

Like unmarried people with a heterosexual orientation, people with a homosexual orientation must learn self-control and chastity (CCC 2359). All unmarried people, whether homosexual or heterosexual, should develop virtue, rely on God's grace to live morally, and avoid situations that will cause temptation to sin (2 Cor 12:7–10; Mt 5:29–30; CCC 2345).

The Church officially teaches in its document *On the Pastoral Care of Homosexual Persons* that homosexual acts are "intrinsically disordered" (CCC 2357). It further states that "special concern and pastoral attention should be directed toward those who have this condition [of homosexual orientation], lest they be led to believe that the living out of this orientation in homosexual activity is a morally acceptable option. It is not" (Article 3).

Scripture condemns homosexual activity: "Therefore, God handed them over to their degrading passions. Their females exchanged natural relations for unnatural, and the males likewise gave up natural relations with females and burned with lust for one another. Males did shameful things with one another and thus received in their own persons the due penalty for their perversity" (Rom 1:26–27). Other verses include Leviticus 18:22 and 20:13, Genesis 18:20, and 1 Corinthians 6:9–10.

There are factors that can diminish a person's blameworthiness for homosexual acts, although nothing can ever make homosexual acts morally acceptable. Homosexual acts violate the moral law. The Bible teaches that the sexual differences between men and women are divinely willed (Gn 1:27–28; 2:24; 5:2; CCC 1604–5). Man and woman are to become one flesh. This refers to more than just the sexual act. It also refers to the natural end result of sexual activity—a baby.

A baby is the direct result of the two becoming one. It has aspects of both the father and the mother. Homosexual sex can never result in a baby. It can never fully achieve the "one flesh" that our sexual power is intended to achieve. Therefore, the moral law, written by God, implicitly condemns homosexual activity.

Pastoral care and compassion should be extended to those suffering from homosexual tendencies. Those interested in more information should read *The Truth About Homosexuality* by Fr. John Harvey, O.S.F.S., which is listed in the Resources section.

Question #172

"If we are supposed to accept others as they are, why does the Church try to change homosexuals?"
Jody G., 16

A. We are supposed to love everyone, but if someone is sinning we are not only *allowed* to call them to repentance but are *required* to do so (Gn 4:9; 2 Tm 4:1–5; Rom 10:14–17; CCC 2358, 2472).

St. James says that if we lead someone to the truth, we not only assist in their salvation but in our own as well (Jas 5:19). Helping someone leave the homosexual lifestyle is actually a great act of charity for two reasons:

1. We are leading them from a lifestyle that is spiritually dangerous. The Bible clearly states that practicing homosexuals will not inherit the kingdom of God (1 Cor 6:9–10).

2. Homosexuality is also physically dangerous. And this is due to more than just the AIDS epidemic. According to a recent (1999) University of Chicago study, homosexual men and women have much higher rates of sickness, suicide, alcoholism, and depression. And in locations where homosexuality is more widely accepted, the numbers are actually higher. This refutes the notion that the mental problems of the homosexual are caused by society's condemnation of the lifestyle.

We can conclude that any effort on the part of people in the Church to help homosexuals lead chaste lives is an act of love.

Question #173

"If gay people are sinners, should we hate them?"
Tom S., 14

A. Jesus said, "Let the one among you who is without sin cast the first stone" (Jn 8:7). We all sin to a greater or lesser degree (1 Jn 1:8, 10; Rom 3:23). If we are supposed to hate and even kick out members of the Church who sin, there would be no one left. Be thankful there is forgiveness. Scripture also says, "But if you do not forgive others, neither will the Father forgive your trespasses" (Mt 6:15).

We are supposed to hate the sin but not the sinner. We are allowed to bring sin to someone's attention and call him or her to repentance, but this is to be done in a spirit of love and humility (Lk 24:15–17).

Question #174

"If being a lesbian or being gay is wrong, why did God make people this way?" Luis C., 14

A. God *permits* some people to have a homosexual orientation, but this does not mean God created them that way or wants people to engage in homosexual acts. God also permits some people to have leukemia or schizophrenia. Does that mean these things are good in themselves?

The fact is that we live in a world damaged by sin (Gn 3:14–19; Rom 5:12–19; CCC 408). God is correcting this through the teachings and sanctification offered by Christ through the Church (Rom 8:22–23; Rv 21:1–5). But He allows bad things to continue for a time in order to bring an even greater good from them (Rom 5:20–21; CCC 312, 324).

God can use things like physical sickness, mental illness, and conditions like anorexia and homosexuality as means to helps us grow in holiness (2 Cor 12:9; Mt 5:3–6). Yet that does not make them good in themselves. The person with a physical weakness for alcohol cannot say, "God made me this way, therefore I can get drunk." Similarly, the homosexual person cannot reasonably argue, "God made me this way, therefore I can act on my orientation."

Many of us find strong tendencies in ourselves, sexual or otherwise, to act in certain ways. Imagine what would happen if we decided to act on these impulses using the "God made me this way so I can act this way logic" of some homosexual activists? Almost anything could be justified (Rom 6; 1 Pt 5:8–9). The alcoholic, the petty thief, or even the child molester could excuse everything with "God made me like this."

You should also know that there is no conclusive scientific evidence that God made homosexuals with that condition. The studies which have claimed a genetic cause of homosexuality have been found to have fundamental problems. On the other hand, most Christian and non-Christian psychologists agree this disorder is not chosen by the homosexual person. There is considerable evidence that homosexual orientation develops because of situations in early childhood. For more information on these points, I recommend Fr.

John Harvey's book *The Homosexual Person* (Ignatius Press).

Dr. Joseph Nicolosi, a Los Angeles-based psychologist, has found excellent success in helping homosexuals rediscover their true heterosexual identity through "reparative therapy," a form of counseling that addresses past disturbances in the emotional and psychological formation of young children. His work is detailed in his book, *Healing the Homosexual*.

Also, Dr. Elizabeth Moberly, a British psychologist, maintains that homosexual behavior is due to difficulties in parent-child relationships. Her study is examined in Fr. John Harvey's book, *The Homosexual Person*. Both Fr. Harvey and Dr. Nicolosi have been ridiculed by the homosexual community, secular psychology, and the secular media because of their studies and implications (Jn 15:18–21; Mt 5:10–12). Nevertheless, their research is quite sound. Their books are listed in the Resources section.

A homosexual person who struggles to be chaste, depends on God, and lives a holy life can see his or her sexual problem as something permitted by God, without inferring that homosexuality is good in itself or that homosexual acts are moral (CCC 2358). As is the case with any serious affliction, homosexuality can be the means to holiness if one turns to God and relies on Him (CCC 2359).

Question #175

"Will God accept you if you are gay?" Nicole W., 14

A. Certainly, if a homosexual person lives a chaste life and does not act on his or her orientation (2 Tm 2:19; Sir 21:1–2). In fact, if a homosexual remains chaste, he or she will surely store up heavenly treasures due to the difficulties they face (CCC 2358). A chaste homosexual is truly heroic, especially in this age when the lifestyle is so widely tolerated and even promoted (1 Pt 2:11; Rom 12:1).

God is love, so in that sense He "accepts" everybody. But He does not accept everything a person does (1 Jn 4:8). The real question is, Will *we* accept *God?* Will we accept His love for us, even if that means giving up whatever sinful lifestyle we have chosen (Mt 5:1–12, 6:19–21)?

The pressure to abandon God's laws is certainly great (Mk 14:38; 2 Cor 11:3; Gal 5:17; CCC 2848, 2849). We should offer anyone struggling with this cross our prayers and support (Jas 5:16; 1 Tm 2:1–3; 2 Thess 3:1–2). Fr. John Harvey's ministry, Courage, and Dr. Joseph Nicolosi's Thomas Aquinas Psychological Clinic in Los Angeles, have had good results in helping the homosexual person rediscover his or her true heterosexuality. I have listed them in the Resources section.

Question #176

"I think I am gay. What should I do?" Adam T., 15

A. Pray and seek solid Catholic counseling from someone who supports the Church's teaching on the subject. Otherwise, you may be given false information. There are many young people, especially boys, who wonder about their sexual orientation.

I recommend you call one of the two ministries listed in the "Resources" section that are dedicated to assisting the person struggling with homosexuality. You will find peace and direction once you understand the cause of the problem and are given a plan of action to work on. I have seen it work in a friend's life and know of a few others who counseling has helped.

Question #177

"Is bisexuality okay?" Justin B., 15

A. No. Bisexuality involves homosexual acts, which are condemned in Scripture (Lv 18:22, 20:13 Gn 18:20; 1 Cor 6:9–10; CCC 2357, 2353). Bisexuality is contrary to the monogamous and heterosexual lifestyle set forth by God. It is no more acceptable than homosexuality or any other sin against chastity.

Bisexuality has become "fashionable" in recent years. This is due to the breakdown of stable family structures, insidious information on television and in the movies, a lack of good moral formation in our schools, and a general breakdown in the morals of society.

Scripture speaks of how lust in man's heart will lead to degrading practices (Rom 1:26–27). Sin fuels more sin. There is no limit to where the sinful human heart can go (Eph 2:3; Rom 1:19–25).

Question #178

"Is it true that the only unforgivable sin is suicide?" Ellie M., 17

A. The only unforgivable sin is the sin against the Holy Spirit (Mt 12:31–32; Mk 3:29; Lk 12:10). And this is the sin of final impenitence, which is the refusal to repent and accept God's grace. The Pharisees sinned against the Holy Spirit because they refused to repent; hence they could not be forgiven (CCC 1864).

Suicide is seriously sinful. Human life is a precious gift of God, and the commandment "You shall not kill" applies to killing ourselves as well as others (Ex 20:13; Dt 5:17). Suicide contradicts the natural inclination of the human being to preserve and perpetuate life. It is gravely contrary to the just love of self, according to the *Catechism* (CCC 2281). One who freely chooses to commit suicide with sufficient reflection and deliberation, knowing it to be seriously sinful, sins mortally.

Even so, many (if not most) people who commit suicide may not freely be doing something they understand to be seriously sinful. Severe psychological factors may be involved in the situation. These can diminish the responsibility of the one committing suicide (CCC 2282).

Also, we should never underestimate God's saving grace (1 Tm 2:3–4). For example, it is said that Jesus appeared to St. Catherine of Siena to tell her that her brother, who committed suicide by jumping from a bridge, had repented before he hit the water. Granted, this story is not a doctrine of the Church, but it offers some hope for the families of those who have committed suicide.

On the issue of suicide, the *Catechism* closes by saying that we should not despair of the eternal salvation of persons who have taken their own lives. By ways known to God alone, He can provide an opportunity for repentance (CCC 2283).

Question #179

"What is the Church's view on the death penalty?" John C., 15

A. Here is the short answer: The Church teaches that the state has the right to use capital punishment, but strongly discourages its use except in very rare occasions. This is because bloodless means are usually sufficient to protect society. The death penalty also tends to contribute to the cheapening of human life throughout society (CCC 2266–2267).

Here is a longer answer: The Church has a long-standing tradition that allows the state to inflict the death penalty to protect the common good, but the state is not obliged to employ this punishment. Biblical passages support the use of the death penalty: Genesis 9:6 ("If anyone sheds the blood of man, by man shall his blood be shed."); Exodus 21:23–25 ("an eye for an eye"); and Romans 13:3–4 ("The ruler ... does not bear the sword without purpose. It is the servant of God to inflict wrath on the evil doer.")

Modern-day Church leaders believe that because morals continue to decline and methods of incarceration today better protect the public, we should work to eliminate the use of capital punishment. Recent popes, including John Paul II, have offered several reasons:

- It is not a deterrent to crime.
- The state runs the risk of executing an innocent person.
- It may prevent the conversion of the convicted.
- It seems to be exercised on a disproportionate number of minorities and low-income people.
- It further erodes society's respect for life.

While Jesus' condemnation of revenge and His call to "turn the other cheek" (Mt 5:39) have been used to encourage the abolition of the death penalty, many biblical scholars believe that (in its original context) this passage refers to individuals, not to the government. Strictly speaking, it would be irresponsible for the government to "turn the other cheek" in its protection of society from criminals and those who pose a danger to justice and order. Nevertheless, we should value all life, including the criminal's. When possible, we should seek to reform the sinner and convert his heart to the loving God (Acts 3:19; 2 Cor 7:10).

Question #180

"In the Bible, it says 'an eye for an eye, a tooth for a tooth.' So why is the Church against the death penalty if a person has committed murder?"
Jody G., 16

A. First, it is necessary to understand the meaning of the Old Testament biblical phrase you mention. Most biblical scholars believe that this was intended to *limit* the retribution one could seek against the person who did wrong to another. It was not intended as an endorsement of revenge but as a demand that the justice fit the crime or offense.

The Church is not against capital punishment in every instance. If bloodless means are unavailable or insufficient to secure the protection of society from murderers then the state can exercise its fundamental right to administer capital punishment to safeguard society (CCC 2265–66).

Regarding the verse you cited, a number of Catholic theologians believe that this law of the Old Testament was superseded with the coming of Christ and the new covenant. They cite Jesus' command to "turn the other cheek" (Mt 5:39) and His warning that if a man lives by the sword, he will perish by the sword (Mt 26:52).

In any event, the Church asks that capital punishment be used only in very rare situations, because it may endanger society's respect for the dignity of the human person, who is made in the image and likeness of God (Gn 1:26–27; CCC 2267). The death penalty can reinforce the culture of death in our society.

Question #181

"Will you go to hell if you are forced to fight for your country in a war and subsequently kill someone?" Adrian A., 15

A. No. Fighting for your country in a "just war" (CCC 2309) is a noble thing to do. Unfortunately, the death of men and women is a tragic consequence of war.

However, if your military superiors order you to do something that is intrinsically immoral, such as executing innocent victims, then you are *required* to refuse by the moral law (Jas 4:17; CCC 2313). You cannot say, "I was only following orders," as many Nazis did at the end of World War II. This will not get you off the hook for doing an immoral act.

Chapter 11

CATHOLIC PRAYER
AND WORSHIP

Question #182

"How do you know when God is talking to you?"
Mary C., 14

A. The more we pray and are silent before God, the more we can know His will for our lives (Lam 3:25–26; 1 Kgs 19:11–12; Prv 3:5–6; Mt. 7:7–11; CCC 2699, 2716). God also reveals His will to us through signs, both small and large. So keep an eye open for unique occurrences, answered prayers, and an overall peace that comes about when you have made good choices (1 Jn 3:19–22).

Most importantly, God speaks to us through His Word (CCC 2700). This Word comes to us in the person of Jesus Christ, who is the Word made flesh (Jn 1:1); through the Bible (2 Tm 3:16–17; CCC 2705); and through Sacred Tradition as handed on by the Church (2 Thess 2:15).

Question #183

"How can you increase your desire to know God?"
Caitlin H., 15

A. Through prayer and study (Jas 1:5–6) and through the sacraments and liturgy of the Church, especially the Mass.

It is through prayer that God will give you the grace to know, love, and serve Him (Jn 5:30; Sir 2:15–17). By studying, you can learn more about God. By worshiping, you come to know and adore Him. When you begin the learning process, you will quickly find that the study of God is fascinating. The more you learn, the more you will want to learn.

Because God is the Author of all things, He knows everything about everything (Jn 1:1–3; Jn 21:17; Acts 17:25). Therefore, the study of God and His interaction with the world *must* be interesting. In fact, I believe the study of the things of God will be the most rewarding endeavor you will undertake.

Question #184

"If one person prays morning, noon, and night, and another person only once a week, does God value His relationship with one more than the other? If so, which one?" Jody G., 16

A. God is closer to those who are closer to Him (Dt 4:29; Lam 3:25). While praying three times a day rather than once a week does not *necessarily* make a person closer to God (one can have the wrong motive for prayer), the person who prays has more opportunity to grow closer to God, all other things being equal.

On the other hand, it is extremely wise to avoid comparing yourself with other people. The Pharisee in Jesus' parable thought he was closer to God than the tax collector praying next to him. But Jesus said that the tax collector was the one justified rather than the Pharisee because he was sincere in his prayer, not simply performing certain actions for others to see (Lk 18:9-14).

Question #185

"If our lives are already planned out by God, why do we try to change our lives through prayer?"
Jody G., 16

A. If you mean that we have no freedom, then, no, our lives are not "planned out by God." God is not "in time"; He is eternal (Jn 8:58; Rv 1:8; CCC 1730, 1732). So, in this sense, He does not know "in advance" what will happen; He simply knows what *is* happening. Every moment is equally "now" to the eternal God—past, present, and future (1 Jn 3:20).

Yet it is easier for our limited minds to think of God as knowing the future. So, we say that God knows what will happen to us tomorrow, but we do not. That does not mean that what happens is not influenced by prayer. For God not only knows what will happen tomorrow, but He also knows your prayer. He can allow that prayer to influence the outcome of things, just as He allows your other actions to shape events (Lk 18:1–7).

Prayer does help determine events. It is like a fork in the road. If you choose a certain path or decision, you will have a certain outcome. If you do not choose a path (that is, do not pray), you may not have the same outcome. So, it is a very good thing to pray. Your prayer will, in many cases, change the outcome of your future (Mk 11:22–24; Jn 14:13–14, 15:7; Mt 7:7–11; CCC 2610). We also believe God helps those who turn to Him in prayer.

Prayer teaches us to direct our lives toward God and to depend on Him. Prayer helps us trust in "providence," which is God's plan for the world and our interaction with that plan (CCC 2633).

Question #186

"Must you make the sign of the cross before you begin any type of prayer?" Charity W., 17

A. No. When you pray, God is looking at your heart more than at your physical actions (Mt 6:5-6). He hears your prayer just as well if you do not make the sign of the cross.

However, we are physical beings, and what our bodies do can affect our spirits. Some actions predispose us more towards prayer, just as certain postures in sports make for a better performance. This is the case with making the sign of the cross. The sign of the cross can prepare us better for prayer.

Because the cross was the means by which the Savior was killed, the early Christians used to make the sign of the cross as a way of recognizing each other in times of persecution. Many of the early Christians write of the value of making the sign of the cross. St. Ephrem the Syrian, in the year 306, said: "Mark all you do with the sign of the life-giving cross. Do not go out from the door of your house until you have signed yourself with the sign of the cross. Do not neglect to make that sign when you are eating or drinking, or going to sleep, whether you are at home or on a journey."

Making the sign of the cross, then, is a holy practice that Catholic tradition upholds. You should try to remember to use it when you pray.

Question #187

"Why are Catholics the only ones who say the 'Hail Mary' and who pray to saints?" Rebecca B., 15

A. Catholics are not the only ones. The Eastern Orthodox Churches and some Anglicans also pray the Hail Mary and invoke the saints.

Why do most Protestants avoid this practice? After the Protestant Reformation of the sixteenth century, some Protestants began to object to what seemed to them to be an unjustified emphasis on Mary and the saints. They thought this emphasis on Mary and the saints caused devotion to Christ to seem less important.

To be fair, there may well have been Catholics who did not understand their faith well and who consequently did have wrong ideas about the Blessed Mother and the other saints. But that was an abuse, and we should not "throw the baby out with the bath water."

The proper response to *wrong* devotion to Mary and the saints is *right* devotion, not no devotion at all. The Blessed Mother and the saints are powerful members of Christ's mystical body, the Church (CCC 2683). As such, they can help us grow closer to Jesus (Heb 12:1; CCC 2683).

Question #188

"What is the use of praying the rosary every day?" Sarah P., 15

A. Faithful repetition of the rosary brings peace to the heart and abundant grace to the soul. Praying the rosary inspires the heart with a more sincere love for the Blessed Trinity and Our Lady. When we meditate on the traditional fifteen mysteries of the rosary, we grow in love and understanding of the joyful, sorrowful, and glorious events in Jesus' life. And anytime we can reflect on Jesus, we are sure to grow in holiness (CCC 2708). (You may have heard that in 2002, Pope John Paul II added the five "luminous" mysteries to the Rosary, bringing the total number of mysteries to twenty.)

You may hear some Protestants say that repetitious prayer, like the rosary, is condemned by Jesus (Mt 6:7). This is not true. What is condemned in that verse is "vain" repetition (CCC 2668). This is meaningless repetition, not meaning*ful* repetition. This verse was condemning a specific ritual of invoking pagan gods with a litany of special names. It is not a condemnation of the rosary, which was not developed for another thousand years. (For more information, go to the website Catholic.com and see Karl Keating's Tract on the Rosary.)

Regarding repetitious prayer, Jesus Himself prayed the same prayer three consecutive times to His Father in the Garden of Gethsemane (Mt 26:39–44). Also, the angels in heaven are continually saying, "Holy, Holy, Holy is the Lord God almighty" (Rv 4:8). Repetition is not condemned, only mindless or vain prayer.

Question #189

"Why is it so important to go to Mass?"
Jeff D., 14

A. The Eucharist is the supreme act of worshiping God because it is Christ offering Himself to the Father on our behalf (Lk 22:19–20; 1 Cor 10:16; CCC 1324, 1365). It is the sacrifice of Calvary made present here and now. By participating at Mass we make Christ's sacrifice our own and receive the grace of salvation anew. When we receive the Eucharist, we receive Jesus Himself (Jn 6:51–59; CCC 1372, 1391).

We have an obligation to worship the Creator (Ps 22:23, Rv 5:13). It would be an insult to receive all the gifts we have received from God (our eyesight, our health, nice home, and so on) and then give Him nothing in return.

Here is an analogy: Let's say God gave a man $168 to live on each week. The man had to pay $56 in rent and $56 for food and living expenses. The remaining $56 would be his to spend in any way. Then let's say that God asked for just $1 of the remaining $56. Wouldn't it be really selfish if the man said "no" to giving God the $1 He requested?

Well, God gives us 168 hours of life each week. We have to go to school or work for approximately fifty-six hours each week, and we have to sleep another fifty-six hours. But then we have fifty-six hours to do whatever we want! Is it not selfish if we do not give Him at least one hour of worship each week (Ex 20:8–11; Heb 10:23–25; CCC 2177–78)?

Question #190

"Why can't they make church services more fun?"
Jennifer M., 14

A. Why can't they make teenagers more serious?

Since when is "fun" the most important thing in life? If someone lives simply to "have fun," that person will end up being very selfish and, most likely, quite unhappy. Focusing solely on our needs is empty and unfulfilling.

It is only when we get out of ourselves and live for others that we truly find peace.

Knowing, loving, and serving God and our neighbor is why we are here on earth (Mt 22:35–40; CCC 1). When one builds their life on the more important things, going to Mass and worshiping God becomes easier. Actually, they become things we really want to do.

Question #191

"Why is Mass boring?" Philip T., 15

A. There are at least four reasons why people, especially the young, are bored at Mass:

1. Many people do not understand what *really* happens at Mass. When we actively listen to the Word of God at Mass, we receive encouragement, wisdom, and guidance (2 Tim 3:16–17). When we receive the Eucharist in a state of grace, we are preparing our soul for its final destination—eternal happiness and peace in heaven (Jn 6:56; CCC 402, 1391). If we really understood the amazing things that happen at Mass, we would have greater interest.

2. Many think they are at Mass to be entertained. They are not. They are there to worship God and give back to Him the honor and glory He is due (Ex 20:1–6, 8–11).

3. Many people have not been taught the faith in an effective manner. Poor catechesis often leads to lack

of concern about the things of God and love for things of the world.

4. We are addicted to excitement and entertainment from watching and listening to too much television and pop music. We are an overstimulated society. The advertising industry knows this. This is why they have reduced TV commercials to as little as fifteen seconds in length. When we begin to slow down, we will begin to appreciate the more sublime riches in life, such as the Mass.

Question #192

"How long before Mass should we abstain from eating?" Jolene N., 17

A. The Church requires that we abstain from eating for one hour before receiving the Eucharist (CCC 1387). Technically, you could eat something before a long Mass and still receive the Eucharist, as long as communion time was an hour after you ate.

The point of the Eucharistic fast is to prepare us to receive Jesus with greater yearning. Fasting before Mass is the appropriate way to prepare ourselves for receiving Jesus. It just doesn't seem right to have a chocolate doughnut or a cheeseburger in our stomachs just a few minutes before we receive the Creator of the Universe.

Question #193

"What should you get out of church (Mass)?" Sean T., 16

A. The real question is, "What should you *put into* Mass?" We are there to worship God (CCC 1070, 1073). He is not there to entertain us. With good and fervent worship of God and heartfelt prayer, you will have an inner peace in knowing that you adore God and are giving Him thanks (1 Jn 4:19; Sir 7:30).

This is the funny thing: People who go to Mass seeking to put in faith, hope, and charity find themselves getting all sorts of wonderful things out of Mass. Those who go trying to get something out of Mass often find it dull.

Chapter 12

MISCELLANEOUS QUESTIONS

Question #194

"Are people ever reincarnated?" Elisabeth G., 16

A. No. Reincarnation is a myth, an idea entirely foreign to what has been revealed by God. The Bible teaches that it is appointed to man to die once and then face judgment (Heb 9:27; CCC 1013). Ultimately, we will go to heaven, to be with God forever, or to hell, which is eternal exile from God's loving presence (Mt 25:31–46; CCC 1022). Of course, on the way to heaven, a person may need purification in purgatory (1 Cor 3:10–17; CCC 1031).

Reincarnation denies the need for a Savior. Titus 3:5 says that we are not saved by works of righteousness, but by the renewal offered by the Holy Spirit. Reincarnation is a philosophy that says we have to continually "work" to improve ourselves, allowing us to come back to life as something better than before. According to this philosophy, the death of Christ for our sins has no meaning because our salvation is totally dependent on our continued work.

Reincarnation also denies the dignity of the person as a unique individual being. You are not really unique if you are the reincarnation of George Washington and, before that, Cleopatra. You are just a recycled person, not the unique "one time" creation made in the image and likeness of God (Gn 1:26–27).

Question #195

"Does the Church believe in life on other planets?"
Andy D., 13

A. The Church does not officially teach anything on the matter. There is no biblical evidence for or against life on other planets. However, if there is life "out there," our God is the God of whatever life exists, for there is only one God (Is 45:5; CCC 290, 300, 2085).

Because God has given us no revelation on this matter in the Bible or Sacred Tradition, many speculative questions can be raised regarding life on other planets. Here are a few:

1. What type of beings are they? (Nearly all scientists who believe that intelligent extraterrestrial life exists say that this life is almost certainly not humanoid— that is, it would be radically different from human beings and, indeed, earthly life in general. These scientists, then, would say that modern science fiction's portrayal of "human-looking" aliens is certainly inaccurate. In their view, no creatures like "ET" are out there.)

2. Did they fall through sin, or are they still in a pristine, unfallen state? If they did fall, they would need to be redeemed by God in some way.

3. Has God revealed Himself to them? Do they have a "bible"?

4. What kind of soul would extraterrestrial beings have? In Christian philosophy, all living beings have a "soul." Human beings have a *rational* soul, which is immortal.

There are many other questions we may ask, but remember: It is entirely possible that human beings are the only intelligent beings in the universe. God could have created things this way. Do not let materialistic scientists throw statistics at you. God is above statistics.

Focus on this fact: The Catholic faith is true, and regardless of what lies "out there," we need to pursue holiness and truth "down here."

C. S. Lewis wrote a space trilogy which considers some of the implications of extraterrestrial life. This might make for good reading if you are seriously interested in the question. The books are *Out of the Silent Planet*, *Perelandra,* and *That Hideous Strength*.

Having said all this, I personally think that the possibility of life on other planets—a humanoid type of life—is extremely unlikely. Why? Because of the way God chose to interact with we humans here on earth. The Second Person of the Eternal Trinity became man (Jn 1:1-18). This is a *monumental,* singular act. It is the ultimate affirmation of *human* life. It seems highly unlikely that the one true God would allow another race to exist in light of this definitive act.

Question #196

"How will I know if God is calling me to the priesthood?" Nathaniel D., 15

A. The first thing I would recommend is that you talk to a few priests and ask them about their vocation. How did they know the priesthood was their calling? Be sure to pray for discernment before and after your conversations with these men (Prv 3:5–6; Tb 4:19).

You should also ask yourself the following questions:

- Do I have an interest in the priesthood?
- Am I interested in the priesthood for my own glory or is my desire for it related to some greater good, such as the salvation of souls?
- Do I find that I have a particular gift that matches the charisms of a particular order?
- Am I detached from worldly things? (This does not necessarily mean that you are against marriage or a career, but that you could sacrifice these for a greater good.)
- Am I attracted to a particular saint and do I have a desire to emulate him or her?
- Do I love the Church and am I willing to sacrifice myself for it and for the laity?
- Do I think I could be happy as a priest?

These are not all the questions you could ask yourself, but the answers to these can give you an indication of whether you have a vocation to the priesthood or religious life.

If you believe you might have a calling to the priesthood, consider going on a vocation discernment weekend.

You are not "signing up" for the priesthood but rather putting yourself in an environment in which you can better discern. This will give you time with seminarians and priests. You will see the positive aspects of the priesthood, which are not often portrayed in the mass media. You will also have the chance to ask questions about the challenges priests face, including celibacy, and be able to pray in nurturing surroundings.

Be sure to consider a religious order or diocesan program that is supportive of Church teaching. The future Church is one that is orthodox in its theology and dynamic in its application. Pray for discernment and choose carefully.

Question #197

"Do you have to follow a vocation if you know you have one? Are there consequences if you do not?"
Caitlin H., 15

A. Everyone has a "genuine vocation," so it is not a question of *if* you have one, but *what* it is (CCC 3). At the very least, we are all called to the general vocation of holiness (CCC 2013). What we typically think of as vocations—married life, priesthood, or religious life—are simply the specific ways we are to fulfill the universal vocation to holiness.

Deliberately opposing or ignoring your vocation can cause problems. Why? Because God has called you to do something and has given you the grace necessary to help you do it. Opposing or ignoring your calling can limit your ability to grow in grace and do His will (Job 9:4).

This does not mean you cannot be saved or that your life will automatically be an irredeemable disaster. But the surest way to lasting peace and fulfillment in this life and heaven in the next is to follow your vocation as best you can discern it (Heb 10:36; Prv 21:30; Mt 7:21).

For example, let us say a man is called to the married life but has a mild fascination with the priesthood and thus, pursues it. Once ordained, he may grow resentful or struggle greatly with celibacy, because he was not meant to live in that state.

Conversely, let's say a man mistakes physical attraction for love and, subsequently, marries. Later, when he has had time to reflect on marriage, he realizes that he was called to the priesthood. He may despair and jeopardize his salvation.

Of course, these extreme situations need not be the case, even for someone who does not follow his true calling. God's grace can overcome even that. But why settle for "Plan B" when God, who is all-knowing and all-wise, has set out "Plan A" for you?

Question #198

"Why are there so few musicians who play contemporary Christian music versus mainstream music?" Kevin M., 18

A. There are at least two reasons:

1. There is more money and fame to be gained in the secular (non-religious) world (1 Tm 6:9–10).

2. Too few young people are committed to the sacrificial life required by Christianity. We will

start seeing more young people get involved with Christian music when we see more young people commit their lives to Jesus Christ.

You will be glad to know that both the Catholic and Protestant Christian music market is growing.

Question #199

"Why can't the Bible be translated into English so that young people today can understand it?"
Joey K., 15

A. It has been. There is a Bible translation called the *International Student Bible for Catholics*.

One problem with Bibles that try to be "hip" or contemporary is that the meaning of some of the texts gets lost in the translation. Translations are sometimes so concerned with being relevant to the young generation that they compromise the integrity of the text. This can be spiritually dangerous in some cases.

You would do well to look for a Bible study that is led by a good priest or youth minister who knows the Scriptures and the Catholic faith.

Question #200

"As a youth, I feel alone and left out of the Church. Are we truly welcome to be a part of the parish family?" Michelle P., 15

A. Yes! According to Jesus, you are not only welcome but of great importance. It was He who said: "Let the children come to Me" (Mt 19:14). Now whether this actually takes place is another matter. I certainly hope your parish is making an effort to reach out to you.

If your parish is like most parishes, the pastor and religious educators are greatly concerned about the spiritual, mental, and physical well-being of youth. After all, you are the future of the Church.

If there are no specific programs for youth, I suggest you get together some like-minded friends and meet with the pastor. He will appreciate your enthusiasm and welcome your assistance in getting something started.

Acknowledgments

Many thanks to **Mark Brumley**, M.T.S., who spent many hours editing the book. You are a good friend and a skilled theologian.

Thanks also to my **mother** and **father**; to my brother **Albert Pinto** for laying the theological foundation; to **Michael Flickinger**, M.Div., M.S., **Fr. C. John McCloskey**, S.T.D., **Patrick Madrid**, **Dr. Edward Peters**, J.C.D., J.D., **Brian Paul**, **Brian Butler**, **Brian Simboli**, Ph.D., and **Michael Fontecchio** for technical assistance; to **Mark Ablett**, **Elena Bucchiarelli**, **Charles Harvey**, **Tracy Moran**, and **Lucy Scholand** for editorial and proofreading assistance; and to my friend and brother-in-Christ **Danny Pope**, whose questions and charitable challenges awakened me to the salvation found in Jesus and His Church.

Get a FREE CD!

RAISING AMAZING CHILDREN
by Matthew Kelly

In every moment, your children are choosing
between the-best-version-of-themselves
and some second-rate version.
As a parent, you cannot control them, but you
can encourage, challenge, and inspire them in
the direction of a life lived to the fullest."

-Matthew Kelly

Order online at **DynamicCatholic.com**
or call **513–221–7700**. Shipping and handling not included.

DynamicCatholic.com
Be Bold. Be Catholic.

A Guide to Confession

On the evening of His resurrection from the dead, Jesus appeared to His apostles and gave them the power to forgive all human sins. Breathing upon them, He said, "Receive the Holy Spirit. If you forgive anyone's sins, they are forgiven. If you retain anyone's sins, they are retained" (Jn 10:22–23). Through the sacrament of holy orders, bishops and priests of the Church receive the ability from Christ Himself to forgive sins. It is exercised in the sacrament of reconciliation, also known as the sacrament of penance or simply as "confession." Through this sacrament, Christ forgives the sins that the members of His Church commit after baptism.

When you enter the place set aside for the celebration of the sacrament of reconciliation, the priest may greet you and together you will make the sign of the cross. He may then choose a brief reading from the Bible to help you feel the merciful presence of Christ.

Next, you will begin with something like "Bless me, Father, for I have sinned. It has been (length of time) since my last confession. I wish to confess the following." You then tell your sins simply and honestly to the priest. The simpler and more honest the better! Don't make excuses! Don't try to disguise or minimize what you have done! Most importantly, think of Christ crucified dying out of love for you. Step on your pride and admit your guilt!

Remember, God wills that you confess all mortal sins by name and number. For instance, "I committed adultery three times and helped a friend procure an abortion" or "I missed Mass on Sunday."

This sacrament is not only for the forgiveness of mortal sins. You may also confess your venial sins. The Church encourages devotional confession, that is, the frequent confession of venial sins as a means of growing perfect in the love of God and neighbor.

After you confess your sins, listen to the advice the priest offers you. You may also seek his help and guidance. He will then give you a penance, and ask you to either pray, fast, or perform an act of charity. Through the penance, you begin to make reparation for the harm your sins have caused you, others, and the Church. The penance of the priest reminds us that we need to be one with Christ in His sufferings so as to share in His resurrection.

Finally, the priest will ask you to express your sorrow for the sins confessed in an act of contrition. You can respond with something like: "Oh my Jesus, I am truly sorry for my sins and, with Your grace, make a firm amendment to sin no more." Then, exercising the power of Christ, the priest will give you absolution. As he prays over you, know with the certainty of faith that God is forgiving all your sins, healing you and preparing you for the banquet of the kingdom of heaven! The priest will dismiss you saying: "Give thanks to the Lord for He is good." You respond: "His mercy endures forever." Or he may say: "The Lord has freed you from your sins. Go in peace" to which you answer, "Thanks be to God."

Try to spend some time in prayer, thanking God for His forgiveness. Perform the penance the priest has given you as soon as possible after receiving absolution.

If you make good and frequent use of this sacrament, you will have peace of heart, purity of conscience, and a deep union with Christ in His love for His Father and for all men and women. The grace of the sacrament will cause you to become like Jesus, our Lord, in all you say and do! It will make you a stronger and more committed member of His Church!

In order to receive the sacrament of reconciliation worthily, the penitent (the sinner) must be sorry for his or her sins. Sorrow for sins is called contrition. Imperfect contrition is sorrow for sins motivated by fear of the fires of hell or the ugliness of sin itself. Perfect contrition is sorrow for sin motivated by the love of God.

Contrition, perfect or imperfect, must include a firm purpose of amendment, that is, a solid resolution to avoid the sin committed as well as the persons, places, and things that prompted you to commit the sin in the first place. Without this repentance, contrition is insincere and our confession is pointless.

Whenever you sin, you should beg God for the gift of perfect contrition. Often God gives this gift when a Christian thinks about Jesus' agony on the cross and realizes that his sins are the cause of that suffering. Throw yourself into the arms of the crucified Savior's mercy and resolve to confess your sins to a priest as soon as possible.

When you come to Church to confess your sins, you should first examine your conscience. Review your life to see how you offended the good God since your last confession. The Church teaches that all mortal sins committed after baptism must be confessed to a priest in order to be forgiven. This "precept" or law is of divine institution. Simply stated, this means the confession of grave sins to a priest is part of God's plan and therefore is supported and carried out in the life of the Church. The *Catechism* (CCC 1455) underscores the therapeutic value of confession for all believers.

Mortal sin is a direct, conscious, and free violation of one or another of the Ten Commandments in a serious matter. Mortal sin, also known as grave or deadly sin, destroys the life of grace in your soul. God's grace begins to draw the sinner back to Him through sorrow for sin. He is brought back to life when he confesses his sins to a priest and receives absolution (forgiveness). The Church recommends that Catholics confess their venial sins, which are violations of God's law that do not sever the relationship with Him or destroy the life of grace in the soul.

—Fr. Frederick L. Miller, S.T.D.

Examination of Conscience

The following will help you prepare for confession. If you are not sure whether your sins are "mortal" or "venial," the confessor will help you understand the difference. Do not be shy: Seek his assistance and ask questions! You always have the right to confess your sins face-to-face or "anonymously" behind a screen. The Church wants to make it as easy as possible for you to make a frank, honest confession of your sins. Most parishes schedule confessions on Saturday. You can also make an appointment for confession.

1. I am the Lord your God. You shall not have strange gods before Me.
—Do I seek to love God with my whole heart and soul? Does He truly hold the first place in my life?
—Have I been involved with the occult or superstitious practices?
—Have I ever received holy communion in the state of mortal sin?
—Have I told a lie in confession or deliberately withheld confessing a mortal sin?

2. You shall not take the name of the Lord your God in vain.
—Have I insulted God's holy name or used it lightly or carelessly?
—Have I wished evil on anyone?

3. Remember to keep holy the Lord's Day.
—Have I missed Mass deliberately on Sunday, the Lord's day, or on holy days of obligation?
—Do I try to keep Sunday as a day of rest?

4. Honor your father and your mother.
—Do I honor and obey my parents? Do I care for them in their old age?
—Have I neglected my family responsibilities to spouse and children?
—Is my family life centered on Christ and His teaching?

5. You shall not kill.
—Have I murdered or physically harmed anyone?
—Have I had an abortion? Have I encouraged an abortion?
—Have I abused drugs or alcohol?
—Have I mutilated myself through any form of sterilization?
—Have I encouraged others to have themselves sterilized?
—Have I harbored hatred, anger or resentment in my heart towards anyone?
—Have I given scandal to anyone by my sins, thereby leading them to sin?

6. You shall not commit adultery.
—Have I been unfaithful to my marriage vows in action or thought?
—Have I practiced any form of artificial contraception in my marriage?
—Have I been engaged in sexual activity with a member of the opposite sex or the same sex?
—Have I masturbated?
—Have I indulged in pornographic material?
—Am I pure in my thoughts, words, actions? Am I modest in dress?
—Am I engaged in any inappropriate relationships?

7. You shall not steal.
—Have I taken what is not mine?
—Am I honest with my employer/employee?
—Do I gamble excessively thereby robbing my family of their needs?
—Do I seek to share what I have with the poor and needy?

8. You shall not bear false witness against your neighbor.
—Have I lied, gossiped, or spoken behind anyone's back?
—Have I ruined anyone's good name?
—Do I reveal information that should be confidential?
—Am I sincere in my dealings with others or am I "two-faced?"

9. You shall not desire your neighbor's wife.
—Am I envious of another's spouse?
—Have I consented to impure thoughts? Do I try to control my imagination?
—Am I reckless and irresponsible in the books I read and the movies I watch?

10. You shall not desire your neighbor's goods.
—Am I envious of the possessions of others?
—Am I resentful and bitter over my position in life?

Resources

Here is a list of apostolates, magazines, books, and encyclicals mentioned within this book:

Apostolates and Institutions

Courage, 210 W. 31st St., New York, NY 10001. Website: www.couragerc.net. Founded by Fr. John Harvey, O.S.F.S., this ministry offers support to the Catholic with a homosexual orientation who is striving to live a chaste life.

Real Love, Inc., 191 University Blvd., #335, Denver, CO 80206. Phone: (303) 237-7942. Website: www.reallove.net. Apostolate founded by Mary Beth Bonacci dedicated to promoting chastity and a pro-life and pro-family message through seminars, tracts, books, and tapes.

St. Joseph Communications, P.O. Box 1911, Ste 83, Tehachapi, CA 93581. Phone: (800) 526–2151. Website: www.saintjoe.com. Publishes audio and video tapes by Dr. Scott Hahn, Kimberly Hahn, Bishop Fulton Sheen, Jeff Cavins, Jesse Romero, and many others.

National Association for Research and Therapy of Homosexuality (NARTH) – Thomas Aquinas Psychological Clinic, 16633 Ventura Blvd., Suite 1340, Encino, CA 91436. Phone: (818) 789–4440. Website: www.narth.com. Assists the person with a homosexual orientation to re-discover his or her true heterosexual identity using reparative therapy.

Authors

Chesterton, G. K.—The works of G. K. Chesterton can be found at www.chesterton.org or by writing The American Chesterton Society, 4117 Pebblebrook Circle, Minneapolis, MN 55437. Phone: (952) 831-3096.

Lewis, C. S.—The works of C. S. Lewis can be found at www.cslewis.org or by writing the C. S. Lewis Foundation, P.O. Box 8008, Redlands, CA 92375. Phone: 1-888-CSLEWIS.

Sheed, Frank — Books by Frank Sheed are available through various publishers. Some of them may be ordered at www.amazon.com.

Books and Booklets

100 Answers to Your Questions on Annulments, Edward N. Peters, J.C.D., J.D., 1997, 2004. Ascension Press, P.O. Box 1990, West Chester, PA 19380. Phone orders: (800) 376-0520. Order on their website: www.ascensionpress.com

The Bible and the Catholic Church, Rev. Peter Stravinskas, 1996. Ignatius Press, 2515 McAllister St., San Francisco, CA 94118. Phone orders: (800) 651-1531. Or order on their website: www.ignatius.com

The Catechism of the Catholic Church, 1994. Doubleday, 1745 Broadway, New York, NY 10019. Phone orders: (800) 733-3000. Website: www.randomhouse.com/doubleday

Darwin on Trial, Phillip E. Johnson, 1993. InterVarsity Press, P.O. Box 1400, Downers Grove, IL 60515. Phone: (630) 887–2500. Website: www.gospelcom.net/ivpress. Or it can be ordered at www.amazon.com

Darwin's Black Box, Michael J. Behe, 1996. The Free Press, New York, NY. Available at www.amazon.com

The Faith, Fr. John Hardon, S.J., 1995. Servant Books, Box 8617, Ann Arbor, MI 48107. Order at www.amazon.com

Healing the Homosexual, Dr. Joseph Nicolosi. Write or call: 16633 Ventura Blvd., Ste. 1340, Encino, CA 91436. Phone: (818) 789–4440. Website: www.narth.com

The Homosexual Person, Father John Harvey, 1987. Ignatius Press, 2515 McAllister St., San Francisco, CA 94118. Phone orders: (800) 651-1531. Or it can be ordered at www.ignatius.com

How the Bible Has Come To Us, J. M. Casciaro and J. L. Navarro, Scepter Press, Box 1270, Princeton, NJ 08542. Phone: (800) 322–8773.

If You Really Love Me, Jason Evert, 1999. Catholic Answers, 2020 Gillespie Way, El Cajon, CA 92020. Phone orders: (888) 291-8000. Website: www.catholic.com

International Student Bible for Catholics. Available through the *YOU!* Magazine website: www.youmagazine.com. Click on the *YOU! Mall* link.

Real Love, Mary Beth Bonacci, 1996. Ignatius Press, 2515 McAllister St., San Francisco, CA 94118. Phone: (800) 651-1531. Website: www.ignatius. com.

A Short History of the Catholic Church, Jose Orlandis. Catholic Answers, 2020 Gillespie Way, El Cajon, CA 92020. Phone orders: (888) 291–8000. Website: www.catholic.com

Theology for Beginners, Frank J. Sheed, 1958, 1976. Servant Books, Box 8617, Ann Arbor, MI 48107. Available at www.amazon.com

The Truth About Homosexuality, Father John Harvey, 1996. Ignatius Press, 2515 McAllister St., San Francisco, CA 94118. Phone orders: (800) 651–1531. Or it can be purchased over the internet at www.ignatius.com

Triumph: The Power and the Glory of the Catholic Church: A 2,000 Year History, Harry W. Crocker III, 2001. Prima Publishing, Roseville, CA. Order on-line: www.primapublishing.com or at www.amazon.com

Where We Got the Bible, Rev. Henry Graham. Catholic Answers, 2020 Gillespie Way, El Cajon, CA 92020. Phone orders: (888) 291–8000. Website: www.catholic.com

Why Wait?, Josh McDowell and Dick Day, 1994. Here's Life Publishers, P.O. Box 1576, San Bernardino, CA 92402. Or it can be purchased over the internet at www.amazon.com

Magazines

Envoy, P.O. Box 640, Granville, OH. Phone: (800) 55-ENVOY. Website: www.envoymagazine.com

Encyclicals, Papal Letters, and Declarations

—*Humanae Vitae* (Of Human Life), Paul VI, 1968.
—*On the Pastoral Care of Homosexual Persons,* Congregation for the Doctrine of the Faith, 1986.
—*Ordinatio Sacredotalis* (Apostolic Letter Reserving the Priesthood to Men), John Paul II, 1994.
—*Women: Teachers of Peace,* John Paul II, 1995.

(These documents can be retrieved by visiting www.ewtn.com or at www.newadvent.org. They can also be purchased through the Daughters of St. Paul, 50 St. Paul's Ave., Boston, MA 02130. Phone orders: (800) 836–9723. Website: www.pauline.org.)

Bibliography

Books

—*The Catholic Answer*, Book #2, Rev. Peter Stravinskas, Ph.D., S.T.L., Our Sunday Visitor Books
—*Catholic Replies*, James J. Drummey, C.R. Publications
—*Catholic Sexual Ethics*, Rev. Ronald Lawler, O.F.M., Cap., Joseph Boyle, Jr., and William E. May, Our Sunday Visitor Books
—*The Catechism of the Catholic Church*, Doubleday
—*Chastity, A Guide for Teens and Young Adults*, Rev. Gerald Kelly, S.J.
—*Everything You Ever Wanted To Know About Heaven*, Peter Kreeft, Ignatius Press
—*The Faith*, Rev. John Hardon, S.J., Charis/Servant Books
—*Hell*, Rev. F. X. Schouppe, S.J., TAN Books
—*Knowing the Truth about Heaven & Hell*, Harry Blamires, Servant Books
—*Purgatory*, Rev. F. X. Schouppe, S.J., TAN Books
—*Purgatory and Heaven*, J.P. Arendzen, D.D., Canterbury Books
—*The Question Box*, Rev. Bertrand L. Conway, C.S.P., Paulist Press
—*Radio Replies*, Vol. 1, 2, & 3, Rev. Leslie Rumble, M.S.C., Ph.D. & Rev. Charles Carty, TAN Books
—*Reincarnation: Illusion or Reality*, Rev. Edmond Robillard, O.P., Alba House
—*The Saint Joseph Baltimore Catechism*, Rev. Bennett Kelley, C.P., Catholic Book Publishing
—*Theology for Beginners*, F. J. Sheed, Servant Books
—*Why Wait?: What You Need to Know About the Teen Sexuality Crisis*, Josh McDowell and Dick Day, Here's Life Publishers

Booklets/Lectures

—*Believe Well, Live Well*, Marianne K. Hering, Focus on the Family
—*A Christian Looks at Mormonism*, Rev. William J. Mitchell
—*The Devil: Does He Exist and What Does He Do?*, Rev. Delaporte, Society of Mercy
—*Do We Believe in the Devil?*, Rev. P.J. McHugh*
—*Eternal Life in Paradise*, La Civilta Cattolica

—*Evolution: A Catholic Perspective*, James B. Stenson, Scepter Books
—*The Great Promise of Our Lady of Fatima*, Daughters of St. Paul
—*How the Bible Has Come To Us*, J.M. Casciaro and J.L. Navarro, Scepter Booklets
—*Is There Really a Devil?*, Rev. William P. Saunders
—*John Corapi's Amazing Story*, Rev. John Corapi, The Mary Foundation
—*On the Pastoral Care of Homosexual Persons*, Congregation for the Doctrine of the Faith
—*The Papacy: Expression of God's Love*, Knights of Columbus, Catholic Information Service
—*Scriptural Texts for Catholic Doctrine*, John Francis Coffey
—*Teen Sexuality*, Barbara McGuigan, St. Joseph's Communications
—*Was St. Paul Sexist?*, Marie-Eloise Rosenblatt, R.S.M., and Ronald D. Witherup, S.S., Catholic Update
—*Watchmaker Newsletter*, Catholic Origins Society, Rev. David Becker
—*What Does the Maleness of Jesus Have to Do With Priesthood?*, Bishop Elden F. Curtiss, Helena, MT
—*What Heaven and Hell Mean to Me*, Rev. Francis Ripley
—*What the Devil!*, Nicholas Halligan, O.P.*
—*When God Calls*, Federico Suarez, Scepter Books
—*Why Do Catholics...?*, Rev. Paul Stenhouse, M.S.C., Ph.D.
—*Why Women Can't Be Priests*, Mary DeTurris*
—*Women: Teachers of Peace*, Pope John Paul II

* These articles were published on the EWTN website—www.ewtn.com

Index

Topic/Question

Abortion, 51, 70, 75, 140, 149, 150, 161, 162+
Abraham, 17
Abstinence from meat, 56, 131
Adam and Eve, 18, 195
Adonai, 63
Afterlife, 118, 194; what will it be like, 108; why people are afraid of death, 109
American Family Association, 172
Angels, 141, 142, 144; as neither male nor female, 141; as guardians, 143
Anglicans, 187
Animals, cruelty to, 65; dominion over, 65
Anointing of the sick, 117
Annulment, 90, 93, 94, 95
Anti-Catholic, 46
Antichrist, 124
Apparitions, 122
Apostolic succession, 23, 37
Artificial birth control (see contraception)
Artificial insemination, 153
Ascension, 122
Baha'i, 41
Baptism, 35, 40, 56, 73, 74, 75, 78, 85, 88, 89, 102, 106, 105, 106; of desire or blood, 106; washes away venial sin, 133
Beatific Vision, 6, 112, 118
Beatitudes, 96, 97
Bible, alone (see *sola scriptura*); as inspired by God, 22, 23, 130; as word of God, 26; authenticated by Church, 23; historicity and reliability, 25; how it developed,

Topic/Question

22; difference between Old and New Testaments, 22, 24; private interpretation, 36; the study of, 46; the canon, 23, 36; translations for youth, 199
Big Bang Theory, 16
Bishops, living in luxury, 54; corruption of, 54; duties of, 88, 128, 130
Blessed Damien de Veuster, 135
Blessed Juan Diego, 125
Blessed Virgin Mary (see Mary)
Bonacci, Mary Beth, 161
Boule, Marcellin, 21
Buddhism, 50
Capital punishment, 179, 180
Carmelite, 146
Catholic, commitment needed to be a, 56, 57; living the faith, 60, 66, 67, 68, 72; how to become a, 40; "unconscious" or unknowing, 104; why be a, 35
Catholic Church, and politics, 39, 51; as the true Church, 37, 38; calls us to holiness, 55; corruption of, 36; established by God, 41; history of, 36; lasting until the end of time, 41; negatively portrayed in media, 55; precepts of, 56; unity of, 44; wealth of, 53
Catholicism, and scripture, 37; apathy towards the faith, 68, 70; contains fullness of revelation, 38; debating for the faith, 69; passing on the faith, 69
Celibacy, 135, 197
chastity (chaste) 164, 169, 170, 171, 174

Topic/Question

Topic/Question

Looking for a Local Catholic Store that Offers **Ascension Press** & **Beacon Press** Books and Resources?

Visit… FindaCatholicStore.com.

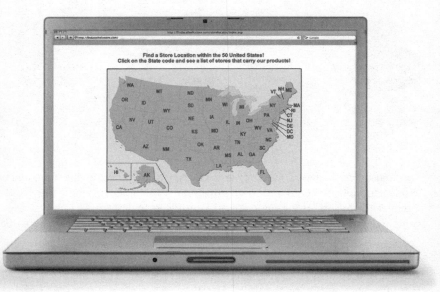

Do you know of a Catholic bookstore that is not listed on this site?

Call 1-800-376-0520 or email info@ascensionpress.com to have a store listed on FindaCatholicStore.com.

Inside: The Truth about Love and Sexuality

Imprimatur
*Pages: **108** • Price: $**11**.99*

Theology of Her Body and *Theology of His Body* are two books in one. Not only will you learn the truth about your own body, but sneak a peek in the other half and discover the beauty of the opposite sex, for it is in seeing the how the two sexes complement each other that one discovers the real meaning of his or her own body.

Theology of Her Body and *Theology of His Body* will give you liberating answers to the most pressing questions about love and sexuality. These books offer solid, real, and relevant points in everyday language about the world you see every day. But more than just presenting the truth itself, they deliver the tools needed to achieve the greatness for which you were created. One thing is certain: anyone who reads these books will never look at his/her body, or anybody, in the same way again.

In these books, you can discover:

- How to live a life that will make you happy and fulfilled.
- That your sexual desires are good and holy and actually designed by God.
- The amazing meaning of your body and that it is very good.
- Your true calling and purpose in life.
- How to be the man or woman of greatness you are destined to be.
    …and much more!

AscensionPress.com • 1-800-376-0520

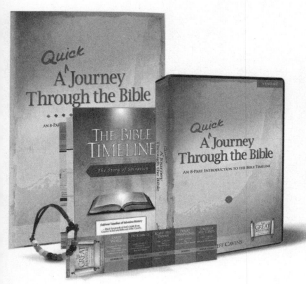

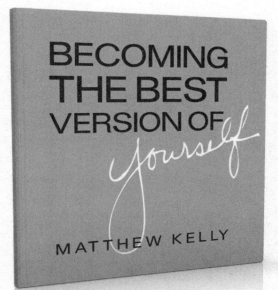

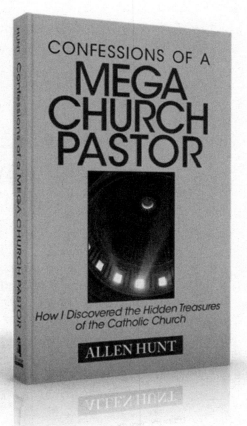

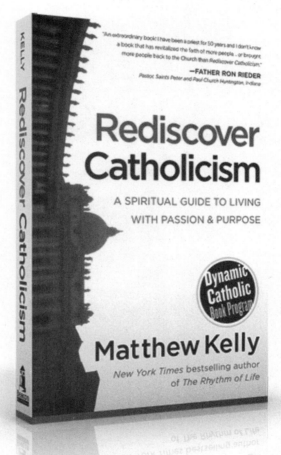